HOW TO PUT
ANXIETY
BEHIND YOU

Robert M. Nideffer is also the author of
The Inner Athlete

Roger C. Sharpe is also the author of
Pinball!

HOW TO PUT *ANXIETY* BEHIND YOU

Robert M. Nideffer, Ph.D.
and
Roger C. Sharpe

STEIN AND DAY/*Publishers*/New York

First published in 1978
Copyright © 1978 by Robert M. Nideffer and Roger C. Sharpe
All rights reserved
Designed by Ed Kaplin
Printed in the United States of America
Stein and Day/*Publishers*/Scarborough House,
Briarcliff Manor, N.Y. 10510

Library of Congress Cataloging in Publication Data

Nideffer, Robert M.
    How to put anxiety behind you.

    1. Anxiety.   I.   Sharpe, Roger C., joint author.
II. Title.
BF575.A6N53   152.4'34   77-20122
ISBN 0-8128-2432-6

To
Alice Fixx
for putting us together,
to
Peggy
who fed us in the throes
of creation
and to
Ellen
who did all the typing.

Contents

Introduction

We live in a society that demands excellence. From the day we are born we bear the expectations of family and friends. No matter what our endeavors may be, we feel the pressure of those who are quick to make judgments. And if that isn't bad enough, we add our own internal demands.

Under the stress of trying to perform our tasks at increasingly higher levels, how can any of us cope with the strain of surviving in the 70s and beyond? This book doesn't offer clear-cut answers or surefire solutions to those problems. But there is a way not to feel overwhelmed by the world we live in.

The obvious goal is to try to control the anxiety that plagues each of us. In an attempt to deal with these anxieties and daily stress many of us have tried a whole range of therapies and procedures readily available in this "self-help" era.

From every direction experts enjoin us to get ourselves together. What is "together"? No one is giving the answer. Instead, the book racks creak with writings on procedures and "new" techniques borrowed from older disciplines. We are told that we can be our own best friend; that open marriage is possible; that it's easy to live with another person; and that if I am ok, you *must* be ok. We're told the only way to truly care is not to care; the way to be active is to be passive, and so much more that it's enough to confuse even the strongest.

Each therapy or suggestion is in its own way an attempt to restructure existing attitudes and lifestyles into a form more able to meet present demands. Admittedly, the cornerstone to this entire movement is a desire by each of us to gain more control over ourselves and our environment. The promise is for more meaning in life, less anxiety and freedom from isolation, and anything that offers to excise our insecurity is warmly received.

Each of us lives with stress and pressure, no matter who we are or what we do. It may be self-generated pressure to succeed, or be different, or even to garner the love of others. Or it may be externally generated pressure from a complicated society, an authoritarian boss, a demanding spouse, overprotective parents or from the expectancies of friends.

We have put so many performance demands on ourselves and our relationships that competition, even self-imposed, has become the key motivation as we try to outdo past endeavors, beat our opponents or simply find a way to thrive. We live our lives within a pressure cooker that saps our energies and affects every aspect of our life. And the dismaying fact is that stressful and pressure-filled situations are here to stay. Society will not become less complicated, less demanding or less threatening. The vital question is how to cope once you accept this, since each of us still has to function and accomplish certain goals. Unless you're ready to "drop out" there seems to be no way to escape. But there is a way to cope that goes beyond blind attempts to get help from one new therapy after another.

That's what this book is all about; to explore some of the different methodologies that are available for helping you reduce anxiety, pressure and the symptoms that so often accompany the stresses of modern living: physical symptoms such as ulcers, high blood pressure, headaches, back pain, and upset stomachs. And the psychological symptoms of depression, apathy, and panic.

We will be delving into some of the most effective procedures available, tallying up their pluses and minuses to give you an accurate and professional appraisal of their worth. Even more important, we will point out some of the critical factors that make one treatment approach more effective for a given person or situation than another. There will be case histories and other examples to help you find the best approach for you.

Our goal is to educate you concerning the therapies that millions have drifted into. Since stress and anxiety are *real* problems we will hone in on those procedures that can alleviate some of the weight you're probably carrying on your shoulders. Attention will be directed to procedures that you can do on your own or with a minimum of assistance. We will also emphasize those that promise some relatively rapid results.

This book doesn't provide a simple solution for a complex problem. Instead, it provides a base for understanding what happens to human beings under pressure, for assessing an individual's strengths and weaknesses, and for using this understanding (of yourself) to design and select treatment programs that fit your special needs. We are not interested in dealing with weekend retreats, or very brief intense experiences that are little more than honeymoons or pleasant (sometimes not so pleasant) diversions. Nor are we interested in telling you about the different types of therapy that cost thousands of dollars and take hundreds of hours of navel gazing.

Our aim in the following pages is to cover comprehensively the following specific areas of concern:

1. What are the long-term consequences of living with stress? And more important, how can you prevent them?

Did you know that many physical, emotional, and decisional problems you may have could be a direct result of stress? Each of us may feel that we handle ourselves well in those situations that cause us to be anxious. We may become so used to their occurrence that we don't even realize the toll they are taking. Nor do we know how capable we would be (and are) when we don't have the excessive pressure to contend with. Perhaps you are aware of gritting your teeth, "smiling on the outside," to repress the fears and pressures you don't want to recognize. Ultimately, the price will be too great. Time and again individuals suffering from hypertension, depression or chronic physical ailments are paying for the growing anxiety that has been chipping away at them over the years.

It is an area of trouble that is easy to spot, once you know the warning signs such as high blood pressure and headaches. One of our goals is to list the things to be on the lookout for and also to tell you what you can do about them through practical applications of available procedures. This early detection is critical if you are to prevent serious problems later, as well as help you function more effectively now.

2. What procedures should you select to be happier with your life and to enhance your own abilities?

We're going to be telling you about a variety of different therapies. If you have a specific problem in your life, it is probable that one approach will be better suited than another. We'll give you a picture of the basic techniques that are being employed and tell you what you can expect from each one. It seems that many shades of gray have developed in the differences between individual approaches. It's a confusing issue to determine the truth and the actual benefits you should or shouldn't expect. We'll tell you how to judge.

3. With all the various techniques available, which directly apply to stress and tension?

Misconceptions abound in the area of new psychological methods. From Silva Mind Control to EST to Rolfing, there are literally dozens of pop therapies that offer their own solutions. The big thing is to understand which are better suited to dealing with the problems of stress. Which offer solutions that allow you to stay involved, and which alter your attitudes and thinking while attempting to change your basic life style and philosophy.

4. What can I expect to pay in terms of money and time? How much must I invest to accomplish my goals?

The emphasis here will be on helping you define your own needs well enough in advance so that you can accurately assess the need for outside involvement (in the form of a professional or trainer) and the length of time training is likely to take. This in combination with information about costs will give you a realistic idea of what is involved. Such knowledge is critical for evaluating the promises that various therapists and gurus are offering.

5. If you need outside assistance, we will tell you how to evaluate what is being offered. What questions should you ask? What promises should you watch out for?

How can you tell a high-pressure salesman from a genuinely concerned therapist or helper? Even more difficult to evaluate is the ability of a sincere person to help, when that individual may be caught up in his own way of viewing the world, thus causing him to apply it blindly to everyone that comes along. When you're under pressure it's difficult to be objective. We'll provide the necessary information you'll need to know.

6. If you haven't found a technique that suits you, don't lose heart. We'll tell you how to combine and modify approaches in order to develop your own treatment program.

Sometimes it's difficult to relate to a predetermined environment or methodology, so we'll offer an added dimension. More than a simple do-it-yourself technique, this final alternative will give you realistic, valid steps to follow. Through all of this our concern is to supply you with a wealth of information in the hope that this can be your source book, a guide enabling you to better cope with stress and pressure. We'll be giving you material to refer to no matter what your needs may be. The important thing is that we'll direct you toward being able to change those parts of your life that you feel are holding you back in getting the most from your day-to-day living.

The following pages will endeavor to accomplish much in getting you in control of yourself and your own capabilities. Whether it is in terms of your career or of interpersonal relationships in your private life, we'll give you the tools that should make you able to achieve greater results and longer lasting satisfaction, no matter what the situation may be.

So sit back and relax. Open yourself to what you're about

to read—and judge everything on its own merits. You're the one who will ultimately decide what's right for you. Our task is to make that choice easier. We know we can. Your anxiety factor is something to be understood as well as controlled. You have the power to put anxiety behind you; all you have to do is believe in yourself. It's that simple.

First, it's important to accept and understand the fact that fear and anxiety play large roles in shaping our lives.

Take that friendly weekend game of tennis, that hand-to-hand combat that calls on most of your physical and mental resources. Does it always remain a game? Or does your mind build it up into something else? Are you suddenly the local Connors or Evert volleying for the championship? Too often, in competitive sports, we begin to play with a vengeance and lose sight of our real physical abilities. We strain to push ourselves beyond the limit and, by so doing, play far under it instead. We get frustrated when reality gets in the way of fantasy and the ball won't bounce where we want it to. If we had just "laid back," it would have been so much better, yet somehow we couldn't.

Perhaps you don't approach the game thinking you're a pro-calibre player. Instead, maybe you're afraid to take a chance because you don't want to look foolish. You pat at the ball instead of swinging through as you do when you're just vollying. Your anxiety tightens your muscles, causing you to feel off balance, clumsy, and uncoordinated. Whatever skills you do possess are negated, and you begin to press. You over-shoot the ball, find your timing off, and begin to question why you're even on the court. The problem is a common ailment of the week-end athlete.

If these weekend stresses weren't enough, we face far more real pressures the other five days of the week. At work the problems may not be readily apparent until we find ourselves facing the subject of the long overdue raise or the young executive with sights on our position. Things become far less secure, and with luck we are able to function without unraveling, but it is a difficult task to remain in control and rationally sort out where we stand.

When the workday ends and we find ourselves on our own time, other problems tend to reveal themselves. An advertisement asks, "How's your love life?" and people laugh, but it really isn't that funny. Interpersonal relationships and sexual interactions can be a far sterner test (and potential source of pressure) than anything else we experience. The fear of rejection or inadequacy can be a devastating occurrence to the most self-assured person. We see the wife worried that she is unattractive and wondering if her husband will stray. We see the husband noticing his middle-age spread and becoming threatened by his wife's outside interests. The power struggles inherent in any relationship and the realities of growing older can be taxing and ultimately self-defeating.

All of these, plus too many others, are areas that can push anyone to their limit. The sensible solution is to lessen the pressure, which can be accomplished if you understand the reasons behind why you feel, and act, as you do in stressful situations. A basic understanding of human responses to pressure is necessary for control. We aren't talking about a struggle to understand the deeply hidden, unconscious motivations that are referred to in the writings of Freud and the psychoanalysts. We are talking instead about what happens emotionally and physically to a person under pressure, independent of what caused it or why. It is this basic understanding of your own responses that is the key to greater physical and emotional control.

Before we go any further in the discussion of stress, it's important to discriminate between *stress,* which we'll define as a situation that offers the possibility for eliciting arousal (physical changes), and *anxiety,* which we'll label as psychological worry or fear. It is important to make this distinction since we'll be dealing with both physical and emotional disturbances that occur in stressful situations. As we talk about situations that have the potential for being stressful we will be referring to them as "situational stressors."

Simply stated, a situational stressor (for anyone) can be an actual situation (e.g. coming face to face with a growling dog), or they can be self-generated internal stressors (e.g. a fear of failure that is with you even when you are succeeding). Previously we gave a few examples of those situations that could become stressful depending upon how you view them. There are of course others, and our responses to these situations determine whether they are actually stressful or not.

Your response to stress can take shape in almost any situation. The important business meeting, the final exam, asking someone for a date for the first time, trying to accomplish routine household activities when others are under foot, a family trip in the car, social functions . . . the list goes on and on. As a preparatory step to helping yourself, it will be important to become aware of those particular situations that you find stressful.

When you are confronted with a particularly stressful situation, you're likely to respond in either of two different ways. There are both physical responses and mental or cognitive ones. Although most of us have both kinds of reactions, it is possible to respond only physically or only mentally.

The physical responses reveal themselves through some easily recognizable symptoms. As the intensity of the stress increases we may begin to perspire freely; feel a surge of adrenaline that surfaces in the form of a sudden flush; our mouth may become dry, and we may even become nauseated. Depending upon our ability to cope we may find our breathing becoming more rapid, causing us to hyperventilate and experience heart palpitations or flutters. Peripheral blood vessels are apt to constrict resulting in cold clammy hands and feet. Our muscles may begin to tighten, causing us to feel jerky and uncoordinated. Tension can even become so high that it begins to be painful, ultimately leading to cramps, headache, and fatigue.

On the other side of the coin are the mental responses that we've labeled as being "cognitive." Stress seems to cause an involuntary narrowing of our attention. This constriction reduces our ability to comprehend and analyze fully what is going on around us. Under normal non-stressful circumstances we may feel comfortable dealing with four or five things at the same time. Under stress this ability is reduced. If the situation is unrelenting in the amount of pressure, then we begin to fall apart in terms of our ability to perform effectively. Simply stated, as the demand to respond to more than we are capable of increases, we begin to feel anxious and out of control. We sense that things are happening too quickly, and we can't meet the pace.

Under this kind of pressure we're likely to respond in one of three ways: 1) Some of us become impulsive and react without fully analyzing the consequences. The businessman buys a hundred shares of worthless stock; the girl on the date agrees too quickly. 2) Some of us refuse to respond. We are so concerned about the possibility of making a mistake that we freeze. Our problem is that we lose out on the golden moment. 3) Some of us respond to the pressure in a very stylized, rigid manner. This could be the senior executive who is out of touch with the times; when threatened by new situations he reacts in the old ways. It makes no difference that the old rules no longer apply.

A second thing can happen to our attention, provided we have also begun to react to the pressure physically. As our heart beats out of control and our mouth becomes dry, breathing patterns change so that we become distracted by our own feelings. Our attention becomes directed inward toward what is going on in our body. We may begin to feel, "I must be anxious, perhaps I am falling apart." The worry builds. The end result is utter chaos that builds and feeds on itself. Performance suffers, we fail, and generate even more stress, depression, and feelings of worthlessness. What was a self-imposed reaction to a situation suddenly has a base of reality behind it. We *are* a failure.

Performance deficits occur because of those errors that are directly caused by pressure and our responses to it. Sometimes the deficits are readily apparent, as is the case if we're competing in sports. Our timing may be off, our coordination may be impaired. It is hard to hide the fact that you tripped over your own feet or ran the wrong way.

The loss of the tennis match may be forgotten with the arrival of the next week's play, but sometimes the results can be more serious. Take the resident in surgery who is being watched by his peers as he performs a delicate operation. Unfortunately, what may happen is that his concentration is split between his patient and those observing his movements. He may become nervous and overly stressed even though the procedure may be something he has performed a hundred times. With no margin for error, the surgeon may suddenly lose control of the situation and unravel, only because he begins to compound the inherent tension in the situation. He can end up cutting something he shouldn't.

Obviously each of us can think of times when we've felt rushed and have seen our effectiveness slip away from our control. The harder we struggle to regain our composure, the more anxious we become. In many ways the mistakes we make compound themselves. We get caught up attending to irrelevant feelings or things around us, rather than responding to the actual activity we're involved with. We rush around the house trying not to be late for an important meeting and wind up stubbing our toe against a piece of furniture, dropping the shampoo, cutting ourselves shaving, or burning ourselves as we drop a cigarette in our lap.

How do you respond mentally when you are under pressure? As you will see later, your response is important in determining the best course of treatment. Take a moment and ask yourself what it is that you do.

Do you become rigid and inflexible? Are you like the quarterback in football who drops back for a pass and looks only for the primary receiver, unable to improvise if that person is covered? Are you impulsive under pressure? Are you like the wife who calls her husband or the doctor every time her child cries, without first taking time to see if that is really necessary? Do you freeze, failing to open your mouth in a social situation or classroom even though you know the answer?

Obviously, there is no suggestion that any one of these responses is better or worse than any other. They all create problems, and our common desire is to reduce the tendency to fall apart in stressful situations.

Up to this point, we have been talking about the acute problems that can develop as a function of your physical and emotional responses to pressure. We have indicated that those reactions can lead to problems or impairment in your ability to respond, and have suggested that these impairments can then become stressful, in and of themselves. Our poor performance is not only upsetting for the moment, but it sets the stage for anxiety in similar situations in the future.

We spoke about a negative cycle that develops within a stressful situation, leading to ever increasing stress and a downward spiral. That same negative cycle can develop as a function of failures, from one situation to another. When this happens, we begin to develop the chronic physical and emotional problems that are associated with tress.

Physically we may begin to suffer from hypertension and high blood pressure. We become more susceptible to problems such as heart attacks and strokes. Psychologically we may attempt to reduce our anxiety by becoming addicted to tranquilizers or alcohol. We may find self-esteem slipping and depression building to the point of contemplating suicide.

The sad case of comedian Freddie Prinze probably bears this out more than anything else. A 22-year-old man "with his whole life ahead of him" was unable to cope with his sudden success professionally and the repercussions of a failed marriage. His only solution, or so he thought, was to take his own life. It is a terrible commentary on what can happen when we feel various societal pressures closing in upon us. The real tragedy of Freddie Prinze was that his death need never have occurred—there were many ways he could have found help.

The young man on a date with a girl he has wanted to see for a long time can elicit a different response. He may become anxious because he sees this as his chance to develop an important relationship. More often than not his nervousness acts against him. He may stammer when trying to talk and become so caught up in his own inability to relax that he fails to see the positive cues that his date may be offering. He reacts under these conditions not to her, but to himself, behaving impulsively becoming paralyzed. The date goes poorly, and he feels foolish. His depression begins, and dates in the future are likely to be worse rather than better.

A parallel true story concerns the physician who was so upset over the fact that he had to tell a pregnant young girl she had leukemia that he could not respond to her emotional needs at all. His own inability to deal with her and death caused him to be rigid. He blurted out that she was dying and at the same time told her she could not carry her baby to term. He told her to go home, to consider abortion, and to return in a week to begin treatment.

He was so caught up in his own emotions that he was unable to empathize with her. He lost sight of the fact she was alone—her nearest friends and relatives were 2,000 miles away. He didn't find out she was unmarried. He didn't even know her religion prohibited abortion. When he discovered that after his talk the girl committed suicide he responded by running from his profession—a second tragedy.

It is easy to see how such events can mushroom and spiral out of control. Admittedly, we've shown extreme examples, but they are governed by the same rules as those little "frustrations" we experience from time to time. You can do something about them. We have the techniques and procedures to teach you control.

Unfortunately, the popularity of, if not the obsession for, tranquilizers in today's world is a sad testimony to our inability to cope with the increasing pressures and tensions of everyday living. Two out of the four most prescribed drugs are tranquilizers. In 1975, the single most prescribed medication in the United States was Valium—a tranquilizer. Think about this fact, mesh it with the hundreds of self-help books, and you begin to understand how paramount the issue of stress is for each of us.

As we all have become more aware of these personal needs there has been a tremendous growth of therapies and methodologies aimed to improve our lives. Unfortunately, they are not all what they seem to be, and under pressure it becomes difficult to separate the wheat from the chaff and evaluate all the options adequately.

Proponents of the various therapies (whose lives economically may hang in the balance) and their disciples (usually "cured" patients) extol the virtues of their particular approach. The pressure these individuals can put on someone who is anxious is tremendous. Selecting your own procedure blindly, or allowing a "true believer" to select it for you, is a little like playing Russian roulette.

Objectively we know better than to believe that one way is the only way, and yet we can see people flocking to weekend seminars and encounter groups with the idea that in two or three days a lifetime of anxiety can be washed away. It isn't that simple a task.

The risk we all take in selecting an approach runs deeper than time or money. We are staking *ourselves* that a therapy might suit our needs, when in truth it may not. It happens frequently that people enter procedures and find that the results are not what they expected, or that they got more (not necessarily good) than they bargained for. It is at this point that defensive mechanisms come into play, or that we get run over by our feelings of inadequacy.

Typically, we react by becoming angry at people for misleading us and consequently lose the trust and faith to try something else that could help. Some of us, under group pressure, go along and become an instant disciple and upset our family and friends. Finally, there are those of us who accept the mismatch as a personal failure. The therapy was right; we were wrong. This interpretation is often reinforced, directly or indirectly, by those involved in the therapy who imply that you didn't give it a fair enough try.

What none of us need is a failed experience to compound the problems we may already be feeling. Since therapy can be very valuable, the people who have been burned when seeking help become unfortunate casualties.

Earlier we mentioned that we were going to focus on those approaches that promise three things: 1) they are specifically used for reduction of physical stress and emotional anxiety; 2) they are useful in helping you deal more effectively with *particular* situations or problems, being focused on well-defined goals; 3) they can be self taught entirely or learned with a minimum of supervision from an expert.

As you can see, our concern is not just with having you cope with stress by reducing it. Rather, our emphasis centers around helping you *manage* stress. Valium and other drugs do indeed reduce the stress that individuals feel. In and of themselves, however, they do not treat the problem. Many of the so call "pop therapies" are little more than diversions and weekend vacations. Like Valium, they too can become addicting and a very expensive habit.

Even after you have selectively reduced the approaches that we deal with, the decision that you must make with respect to which one to use is not easy. TM, biofeedback, hypnosis, or progressive relaxation may produce the same changes in you when they are effective. The rationale behind each of them, however, the problems that they focus on and the personalities of the individuals who are able to use them are all different.

One additional difficulty in selecting a procedure is that most of us need more than one. We mentioned earlier the dynamic nature of the human condition and the fact that there are no easy solutions that fit everyone. Ideally, we should feel free enough to combine different treatments, taking what we will from each in order to gain the insights, support, and skills that we need to improve our lives.

This selection and matching process is critical to our well-being. What is difficult is to be detached from ourselves long enough to be able to evaluate what we really need. There are so many variables making up our personality that this task is sometimes more difficult than we would anticipate. We think you will be in a much better position to make those decisions after reading this book.

The procedures we will be presenting in detail are hypnosis and self-hypnosis, biofeedback, meditation, procedures like those Benson described in *The Relaxation Response*, progressive relaxation, autogenic training, cognitive behavior modification, mental rehearsal, systematic desensitization and implosion. We will also touch more briefly on positive thinking and cybernetics.

All of the procedures have been found to be effective in helping people cope with the stress and pressure of day-to-day living. A major factor in their effectiveness, however, rests with the individual. Are you motivated enough to become actively involved in the therapy? Can you develop the faith and confidence necessary to allow the procedure to work for you?

Faith and confidence are critical words, and we are using them interchangably. The procedures will work if you are able to use them in the way they are presented. For example, TM may require you to attend, in a particular way, to a mantra (the special word you meditate on). The promise is that if you do this in the right way you will find blood pressure and other signs of arousal decreasing. Unfortunately, if you have difficulty developing faith in the procedure you will not allow yourself to follow through. Instead of attending as you should, you will be arguing with yourself, and telling yourself it's not working. And it won't.

Part One

DISCOVERING WHO YOU ARE

1

Self-Assessment

To be effective, a treatment program must respond to both the causes of the problem and to your own expectancies. Unfortunately, it is not at all uncommon for these two elements to be in conflict with each other. Most of us think we know what we want. We're bright, astute individuals who see other people's problems and difficulties very easily. However, the stress we experience interferes with our ability to analyze and see our own problems. We often tend to oversimplify or even ignore our difficulties in coping with life.

By exposing you to a variety of problems through the case histories that will be presented with each procedure, we hope we will sensitize you to some of the things that may be affecting your life. A first step in helping yourself is to get a very clear view of your problem. In the next few pages, we will try to help you examine your own situation more closely. We'll ask questions that should go a long way in enabling you to find an image of your own abilities and talents.

A second important factor involves being able to separate the procedures on the basis of their appropriateness for your particular mental or physical need. This becomes a fairly simple task once you can isolate the cause and effects of the problem you may have, and in these next two chapters we will tell you what types of symptoms different procedures are better suited for.

Deciding whether a particular procedure is the proper technique for a specific problem becomes simple common sense, once you know the cues and secrets in the selection process. It is vital that the treatment fit your personality and needs. Some of the critical factors to consider in selecting a treatment would include the following:

1. The length of time a session lasts.
2. How quickly the procedure works to reduce stress, whether it be seconds, minutes, hours, days, months, or longer.
3. The number of training sessions required for some changes to occur.
4. The cost.
5. The background out of which the procedures developed.
   a. Your expectancy about the procedure based on its history and your attitudes.
   b. The attitudes of key people in your life toward the treatment.
6. The mode of presentation and atmosphere in the treatment setting.
7. Whether your attention is active or passive.
8. Your need for physical activity or your ability to sit quietly.
9. Your need for support and guidance.
10. Your need for control and the focus of control in the procedure. Is treatment under your control, a therapist's, or that of some piece of equipment?
11. The complexity of the theory behind the treatment and your need for a detailed explanation.

12. The complexity of the treatment procedures and how much you must learn.
13. Whether you are asked to attend to things inside yourself or outside in the environment.
14. Is the focus on physical symptoms?
15. Is the focus on attitudes and mental processes?
16. What are the goals of treatment?

It would seem obvious that factors like the ones just presented should influence both selection and design of a treatment program. Unfortunately, this is not always the case. People can become so caught up in their own set of answers or the "pop therapy of the month" that they set rational judgment aside.

The right side of your brain, that part associated with feeling and intuition, is important, but it is only half of the brain. Before leaping in because it feels good, or because screaming, chanting mobs can't be wrong, use the left side of your brain. During the next few pages set emotions aside and try to become more analytical and detached from your own feelings.

Section I: Overriding concerns

As you work through the assessment process you will probably find one or more approaches that seem to be of potential value to you. But there are some practical overriding issues that must also be considered.

1. What are your financial resources? Treatment costs can range from the price you paid for this book to $75 per hour or more. A question you might well ask yourself is, How much am I going to have to invest, and what does my money buy? If two people offer the same service and I know that when effective the outcome is the same, shouldn't I then just take the best bargain?

In terms of outcome it is true that (particularly with the procedures presented in Part I) there is little difference. There are individual selection factors, however, that make some procedures and some trainers or helpers more likely to be effective for you. You should be purchasing two things with your money, and they should both increase the likelihood of success.

The first thing you should be buying is support and reassurance. This will come from someone or something you can place confidence in. Some of us need a person with a title, whether it be priest, minister, Ph.D, M.D., guru, or something else. For others, reassurance comes from something they perceive as more reliable and trustworthy than mere human beings: for example, a piece of equipment that objectively measures what is going on in your body.

The second thing that you should be purchasing with your money is guidance. The more money you spend, the more capable the therapist should be of assessing you as an individual, or understanding your special needs, and of designing an approach that fits you, rather than fitting you to the approach. The type of expertise we are talking about here is not contained in a biofeedback machine, nor in a true believer of any single therapy. The hard-sell individual who has one technique to offer is not for you, whether he is selling TM, est, Primal Therapy, or psychoanalytic therapy. He may be an expert in his special area and also may have a great deal to offer—if you fit into his specialty. He is not the person, however, to help you make an unbiased decision.

In Chapter 13 we will be discussing the issues of where to go for help in more detail. At that time we will give you some hints for selecting a trainer or therapist who will be appropriate and a useful supplement to any self-treatment you're contemplating.

2. How much time do you have? How long can you

practice a procedure before having some major attitude or behavior change? Most of us would like changes to occur almost magically and immediately, but in considering this question you should try to be realistic.

If you want to use what you learn to help yourself cope with a particular problem, how long do you *really* have? Can you take 20 minutes out of a busy schedule to meditate, or do you have to gain control in just a few seconds?

3. What access do you have to outside help? Many rural communities lack professional services and training facilities. Often it is possible for an expert to design a program that compresses training time, or reduces the number of sessions, so that people from "out of town" can participate. For many of you this would be appropriate, but the merit of such a shortened or compressed procedure must depend on your particular problem. Beware of the promises that claim to reduce a normal 20 session program into 5. This is especially true if the person says they can do it without first having found out the details ab ut your problem.

Too often these quick treatments are a waste of time and effort, and you end up throwing your money away. By answering some of the questions that follow, you should be able to get an idea of the amount of time and professional involvement you will need to accomplish your goals.

Section II: Expectancies and Attitudes

Money, time and accessability can be very important limiting factors in selecting treatment. There is a second set of issues that interact with treatment selection as well as influencing length of treatment. These have to do with your own expectancies about the therapy and, if one is involved, about the trainer or therapist. They also have to do with the amount of support you receive from your surroundings.

It may sound silly, but many of us find it very difficult to get involved with, and place trust in, an individual who does not fit our image of a helper. To some, long hair, casual attire and sandals would be so upsetting that we could not listen to suggestions or advice no matter how good they were. To others, a three-piece suit, short hair, lapel pin and membership in the local country club would be equally hard to swallow.

If you remain in the situation long enough, and if the trainer or therapist is competent, you'll overcome these resistances, but this will add to treatment time. By minimizing conflicts before you begin, you can shorten training. The examples presented were rather dramatic, but even subtle things are important. If you are fortunate enough to have several people to choose from, a look at your own expectancies might shorten training considerably.

What do you expect from a trainer?

1. What kind of training should they have had?
2. How old do you expect them to be?
3. What sex can you relate to better?
4. Do you want them to be assertive and directive?
5. Do you want them to be nondirective, leaving decisions up to you and providing support?
6. Should they be warm and supportive?
7. Should the trainer be professional and businesslike?
8. What should they look like?

Don't sell your expectations short. Meditation might be a treatment you need, but if the trainer is a guru-type and you are a conservative Republican you may fight some battles before you get down to business.

What are the attitudes of those around you towards stress-reduction procedures in general and toward the ones you are considering in particular?

1. The people you live with
2. Family
3. Close friends
4. People you work with
5. Teachers

How involved are the above groups in your life, and how much contact do you have with each of them? The more supportive your environment, the shorter and more effective your training is likely to be. Take some time to identify those things you can do to maximize the support systems around you. You might join groups with similar interests. You could begin to educate family and friends so they see your side. If they are too inflexible to listen, then find ways to avoid the issues. Don't flaunt what you are doing unless you can use the criticism and negative reactions of others to motivate yourself to prove something.

Section III: What is your problem?

The approach you choose will be greatly influenced by what you define your problem to be. Take a few minutes to write down a description. This should be something you might give to an individual whom you are planning to have help you. Pay particular attention to:

1. How specific the problem seems to be, both in terms of the situations that cause it, and in the symptoms that result.
2. Whether your reactions to the stress are physical (e.g. pain), and/or emotional and attitudinal.

To help you further articulate the problem, and to improve your sensitivity, we have listed a number of specific symptoms associated with stress. Please check those that apply to you. This information will be important in treatment, both for selecting an approach and for providing a treatment focus or direction. The more focused you become the more rapid a solution can be achieved.

1. *What physical symptoms do you experience?*   Yes   No

    a. I become light-headed and/or dizzy.   ___ ___
    b. I have heartbeat irregularities: fluttering, palpitations, skipped beats.   ___ ___
    c. I get nauseated; stomach upset.   ___ ___
    d. I develop migraine headaches.   ___ ___
    e. My blood pressure increases, and I feel flushed.   ___ ___
    f. I develop muscle tension and pain.
        1. Tension headaches   ___ ___
        2. Cramps   ___ ___
        3. Back pain   ___ ___
        4. Neck and shoulder pain   ___ ___
        5. Tics or twitches   ___ ___
        6. Chest pain   ___ ___
    g. I perspire heavily.   ___ ___
    h. I feel weak.   ___ ___
    i. I hyperventilate and breathe rapidly.   ___ ___
    j. I get a dry mouth and throat.   ___ ___
    k. My movements become clumsy and jerky. I bump into things, trip, burn myself, etc.   ___ ___

2. *What are your emotional responses to pressure?*   Yes   No

    a. I begin to feel uneasy and apprehensive.   ___ ___

Yes   No

b. I feel unsteady and off balance. ___ ___
c. I start worrying about making mistakes. ___ ___
d. I derogate myself, listing my inadequacies. ___ ___
e. I compare myself unfavorably to others. ___ ___
f. I begin to feel a sense of panic. ___ ___
g. I feel as if I am wound up inside and just want to scream. ___ ___
h. I begin predicting my own downfall. ___ ___
i. I feel worthless. ___ ___

In this next part we want you to take some time to trace the history of your problem(s). You may have described your concern as a specific fear about taking an exam or encountering a particular situation. On the other hand, you may have defined it in much more global terms as a general unhappiness or anxiety that seems with you almost all the time. In either case, it is here that we want to find out about your past experiences with the concern.

1. How long have you had the difficulty? _____
2. How frequently do you find yourself upset or disturbed by the problem? (List the number of times per day, week, or month as indicated.)
   a. Times per month divided by four _____
   b. Times per week _____
   c. Times per day multiplied by seven _____
3. How many different situations can lead to the problem?

Although you may have defined your problem as "speech anxiety," or "losing control of your children," there may be several very specific situations that elicit your anxiety. With speech anxiety, for example, you may find that it is aroused by any situation where you are the center of attention. As for your children, are these specific problem areas: trying to get them off to school, making them behave in public (the supermarket, etc.), getting them into bed at night, stopping their interruptions (when you are on the phone or company is present)? List the troubling situations below, and be as specific in each instance as you can.

Section IV: *What are your needs, abilities, and level of motivation?*

1. *What happens to your attentional processes when you are under pressure?*   Yes   No

    a. I begin to feel rushed, as if things were happening more quickly than usual.   ___ ___

    b. I find myself distracted by things going on around me.   ___ ___

    c. I become confused and jump from one thought or idea to another without really tying them together.   ___ ___

2. *What is your need for physical and mental activity?*   Yes   No

    a. It is difficult for me to sit still for any length of time.   ___ ___

    b. I need to be doing something physical almost constantly.   ___ ___

    c. I am on the go from the time I get up until I go to bed.   ___ ___

    d. I don't enjoy being alone with my thoughts.   ___ ___

e. I need something happening to keep me involved. I need to be reading or watching TV if I am just sitting.

Yes   No
___ ___

3. *What is your need for control?*

	Rarely	Sometimes	Frequently	Most of the time
a. I am in control of interpersonal interactions with friends, relatives, etc.	—	—	—	—
b. In school I would not wait for the teacher to finish giving instructions before starting.	—	—	—	—
c. I am usually faster than others at figuring things out.	—	—	—	—
d. I make my own decisions.	—	—	—	—
e. People come to me for advice and guidance.	—	—	—	—
f. I am a leader.	—	—	—	—
g. I am independent and self-sufficient.	—	—	—	—

4. *What is your need for structure?*

a. I don't feel comfortable doing something unless I am sure I have all the information.	—	—	—	—
b. When I go to a doctor I want to know all the details behind his analysis and treatment.	—	—	—	—

    c. I am a disciplined person.　—　—　—　—

    d. I create goals and deadlines
       for myself and stick to them.　—　—　—　—

5. *What is your need for support?*

    a. I seek out other people for
       advice before making de-
       cisions.　—　—　—　—

    b. I select my doctor more on
       the basis of his bedside man-
       ner and concern than for his
       technical competence.　—　—　—　—

    c. I need a lot of reassurance
       and support.　—　—　—　—

    d. I prefer to let others make
       decisions, especially impor-
       tant ones.　—　—　—　—

    e. I enjoy physical contact and
       warmth.　—　—　—　—

    f. I dislike being alone.　—　—　—　—

6. *What is your level of self-esteem?*

    a. I am as capable as most peo-
       ple I know.　—　—　—　—

    b. I am a good person.　—　—　—　—

    c. I give a great deal to others.　—　—　—　—

    d. I am happy.　—　—　—　—

    e. My family is proud of me.　—　—　—　—

    f. People see me as calm and
       capable.　—　—　—　—

    g. I get depressed.　—　—　—　—

    h. I feel worthless.　—　—　—　—

Section V: *What are your treatment goals?*

What is it that you hope to accomplish in terms of reading this book and in terms of applying stress-reduction procedures to your life? The articulation of goals is important. It provides information to help you make the right selection from among the various methods of stress control. It indicates how long practice will be needed in order to effect change. Generally speaking, the more global and all-encompassing the goal you establish for yourself, the more time you will need. Finally, a goal provides structure and definition, while also being a light at the end of the tunnel. This is very important since it will allow you to gauge your own progress as well as making you sensitive to change. In doing these things the goal can provide the support and encouragement needed for successful treatment.

In the questions below some key words are italicized because they influence the selection of a procedure. Goals can be *general* or *specific*, they can focus on *physical* or *mental* concerns, and they can emphasize changes in *attitudes* and/or *behavior*. As you will see in the next chapter, different procedures respond more or less directly to each of these concerns. In the space provided check off each of the goals that apply to you.

1. *What is it you hope to accomplish physically?*   Yes   No

   a. To *prevent* the development of chronic *physical* problems (ulcers, hypertension, stroke, heart attack).   ___   ___

   b. I want to treat a *specific physical* symptom that occurs in a *specific situation.* For

Yes No

example, I want to reduce neck pain from driving in traffic, or I want to avoid tension headaches that develop when I have deadlines to meet.   — —

c. I want to treat a *specific physical* problem (e.g. migraine headaches) that occurs under a *variety of circumstances* that may or may not be stress related.   — —

d. I want to *improve* my *ability* to *perform physically* in a *specific* situation. For example, I want to be able to make the pressure putt in golf, win the key point in tennis.   — —

e. I want to improve my ability to *perform physically across* a variety of *situations, and I want to develop* new *skills.*   — —

2. *What is it you hope to accomplish mentally, attitudinally and emotionally?*   Yes No

a. I want to *prevent* the apathy, depression, loss of enjoyment, motivation, and self-esteem that can occur as a function of continual pressure and stress.   — —

b. I want to *treat a specific problem* (e.g. feelings of inadequacy) when it comes to a *specific situation* (e.g. giving a speech).   — —

c. I want to *treat a general* problem that I experience in a *variety* of *situations.* For example my feelings of inadequacy as a mother, or as a teacher, etc.   — —

d. I want to improve my mental *performance* (e.g. ability to analyze information

Yes No

and make decisions) in a *specific situation*
(e.g. asking for a raise).   ___ ___

In the next chapter we will help you interpret your own
responses. In preparation for this, however, you should
engage in a little bookkeeping and score your answers. The
only areas that require any computation are contained in
section IV (pg. 13) beginning with Part 3.

In Section IV, Parts 3, 4, and 5 are to be scored in the
following way.

Rarely	= 1
Sometimes	= 2
Frequently	= 3
Most of	
the time	= 4

Add the scores separately for Parts 3, 4, and 5 and enter
them below. In Section IV Part 6 the scoring is the same for
items a. through f. Items g. and h., however, are scored in
the reverse direction. Thus a response of "rarely" to item g.
("I get depressed") would receive a score of 4. Add the
scores assigned to each of the items in Part 6 and enter that
score below.

Total Score

Part 3	___
Part 4	___
Part 5	___
Part 6	___

2

Choosing the Procedure That's Right For You

By this time, if you have done your homework, you have checked your pocketbook, looked at your calendar, thought about available resources, and have identified a particular problem. You should also have a pretty good idea of the type of individual you think you can work with (should you decide to do so). In addition, you should know whether family and friends will be helpful, or if they will interfere with what you are trying to do.

Through responding to the questions in the last chapter, you should have a clearer understanding of your problem than you had previously. Now the time has come to decide what to do about it, and the best place to begin is with the questions asking you to identify your physical and emotional responses to stress (Section III).

Examine your answers to Part 1 of Section III. The more you find yourself reacting to stress with physical responses and symptoms, or the more you suffer from physical symptoms even in the apparent absence of pressure, the more sense it makes to employ a procedure that will treat those specific symptoms. Thus biofeedback would be an obvious treatment for headaches, muscle tension, etc.

Likewise, progressive relaxation and hypnotic suggestion can be used.

If the primary emphasis is on worry and feelings of anxiety (emotional responses), then more cognitively oriented procedures should be considered, such as cognitive behavior modification, self-hypnosis or the power of positive thinking.

In the examples just presented we were talking about *specific* symptoms. When the situation creating stress is specific, but your responses are broader (e.g. several physical and/or emotional responses), it makes sense to select a procedure that alters the effect the situation will have. Your aim is to get rid of the symptoms by improving your ability to handle the stressful situation. Under these conditions systematic desensitization, implosion, cognitive behavior or mental rehearsal could be used.

The next section of the test asks you to look at the history of your particular problem(s). As you do, you should keep one thing in mind: The more chronic (long-lasting) and the more global (the more situations affected) the problem, the more likely you are to need some outside help.

In contrast, the more specific the problem and the more clearly it is tied to a stressful situation, the more rapidly you are likely to overcome it. The frequency of the problem is not usually a hindrance. In fact, it is often helpful if you experience it frequently. For example, if you wanted help with migraine headaches but averaged only one headache a month, it would be difficult to tell if therapy was having an effect. When you can see an immediate effect, treatment is reinforced and long-term changes are much more likely.

To minimize the need for outside help and to maximize the likelihood of change, you should isolate your problem as much as possible. Thus, even though there may be a great many situations that make you feel inadequate, try and put them in their order of importance. Then take the situation that is most important to you (e.g. controlling your kids in the market, or giving a particular speech) and work on it.

Nothing can interfere with a stress-reduction program more than being unable to stick to a problem!

The temptation to jump from problem to problem, or to apply a solution to more than one area at the same time, will be great. Don't do it. You will end up splitting your energies and resources, and ultimately not solve any of your problems. Wait until one is under firm control before you tackle the next one.

What are your needs, abilities and level of motivation?

The first questions in this section focused on your attentional processes under pressure. The changes that the questions refer to (distraction, confusion, etc.) are fairly common. If you experience them, it is a good signal that some relaxation procedure would be useful. Notice that although these are perceptual changes, and not what we have been referring to as physical responses to stress, they still indicate a need for a physical-relaxation procedure.

Think for a moment about your answers to the attentional questions. Depending on what it is that seems to be overloading you and making you feel rushed, you'll want to choose your relaxation procedure carefully. For example, if you find yourself getting confused and caught up in your own thoughts, then you'll want the procedure to be one that draws your attention outside yourself. Under these circumstances TM, autogenics, progressive relaxation and self-hypnosis may be more difficult for you to use than biofeedback or hypnosis.

Both biofeedback and hypnosis require that you pay

attention to something outside yourself (the hypnotist's voice, the feedback signal). Additionally, massage and exercise can also be helpful in getting you out of your head. As a final note, it is possible to modify a procedure, such as progressive relaxation, so that you put the procedures on tape. You can then listen to the tape, which helps you to move your attention away from the inner confusion.

If the overload and confusion comes from the outside, you will need to take special care in selecting a place to practice. You will probably want to be able to close your eyes if biofeedback is used, so that the auditory feedback can be better attended to.

You may want a simple procedure that offers some straightforward, simple instructions. TM can be very useful. Open-ended procedures like self-hypnosis and biofeedback (if you are left to your own devices to discover ways to control arousal) may be difficult to use, especially at first.

What is your need for physical and mental activity?

For many of us the most anxiety-inducing experience we can have is to just sit still with nothing to do and with no distractions. Consequently, our activity level will have a great deal to do with how easy it is for us to become involved in a procedure that requires quiet contemplation or restricts physical activity. As you examine your answers to these questions try to see whether mental or physical activity is more difficult for you to restrict.

If you find that your mind is in constant motion and you're always actively thinking about something, it may well be that you need to reduce that tendency. Sitting quietly in a corner, however, is often not the answer. You may have better success if you employ a procedure that allows for some active attention, while also directing you to some non-arousing things. Although procedures such as TM seek to direct attention to a non-arousing mantra, the problem is that there is so little structure, and the mantra itself is such a neutral stimulus, that it may not be able to compete with the over-working of your own head.

If you have difficulty slowing down mentally and physically you can often overcome the problem, not with a head-on confrontation, but by flowing with your own needs. Select a procedure such as autogenics, which is short and structured enough so that the need for physical movement is not interfered with for any length of time. Mental rehearsal and cognitive behavior modification can be used because they both encourage active mental activity.

Exercise classes, Tai Chi, yoga, and massage can also be used. The critical element is to direct attention to enjoyable non-arousing sensations. Some individuals find their own special exercises, such as body surfing or even riding trail bikes. In both these instances, the activity is physically demanding but not threatening. If you tend to get caught up in your own anxieties and thoughts (which is difficult during such activities anyway), you can get banged around by a wave or bumped on the motorcycle. This gets you back outside of your own head. This will alleviate the tendency to turn a pleasant experience into a stressful situation.

What is your need for control?

What was your score for this section of the test? The higher the score (especially if it was above 21) the more important it will be for you to have some say and control in the procedures that you use to reduce stress. Any procedure that involves others—for example, hypnosis—will be facilitated if the hypnotist structures things so that you are given more responsibility. Induction techniques can be used that are controlled by you. Often people who need to be in control seem to respond more quickly to procedures that have a scientific base. Procedures such as biofeedback, progressive relaxation, and autogenic training can be presented in a very straightforward way. In those with a hint of mysticism or the unknown, it is often difficult to trust and relax enough to use them effectively. Thus, TM, hypnosis, and other meditative procedures may be more difficult to use.

If you are one of the many people who needs a fair amount of control, you may also find that you have little patience. If that is the case, it will be important that you are able to experience some effect from training immediately. For this reason alone autogenics may be a little difficult. It is possible, however, to modify the autogenic procedure so that intentional formulae (which fit nicely with a need to control) are still used although practice will have to be extended from 90 seconds to several minutes. This will allow for some marked results but may interfere with your being able to use the procedure in critical situations where you must relax rapidly.

What is your need for structure?

A score above 12 on this section of the test indicates that you are more likely to respond to a procedure that has a convincing explanation behind it. Depending on your own background, that explanation could be religious, mystical, or scientifically based. The critical point here is that you either take the time to satisfy yourself by doing some background reading or rely on the trainer for explanations.

It can also be important to have structure built into the procedure. Autogenics can be good for this because it provides a very concrete, step-by-step set of instructions, as does progressive relaxation. If instructions are too vague—"Just be passive," "Do whatever you can to lower the click rate and reduce tension"—they can generate anxiety. It will be important to have regular practice times, and when a trainer is involved, he should recognize and respond to your need for structure. If he has an extremely casual attitude, he might wind up frustrating you rather than teaching you the things you'll need to know. He can be warm and relaxed, but his main concern should be to provide information and structure.

What is your need for support?

The higher your score on this section of the test, particularly as you begin to move above 12, the more difficult it will be for you to use procedures totally on your own. This will also be true if you have a very low score on the sections dealing with need for control and self-esteem.

Procedures such as hypnosis and biofeedback, which usually require a therapist (at least at first), are often desirable if you have a high need for support. The next best thing would be to select procedures that start with a professional teaching you a technique (e.g. self-hypnosis or TM) and then shift responsibility to you while still leaving the door open for consultation. A third way of proceeding would be to find, or even start, a group that meets on a regular basis and practices together. The major difficulty with this last notion is to keep the group focused on the task of learning the procedures. If you can do this, however, the reinforcement and support you'll provide for each other may prove to be very beneficial. This is the basic principle behind many programs that have enjoyed great success, including AA and Weight Watchers.

What is your level of self-esteem?

The lower your score (less than 16), the more important it will be for you to have positive feedback and support. For this reason procedures that involve other people should be looked at first. For example, biofeedback could be difficult if it were presented in a rather cold, technical way. After all, the equipment doesn't generate warmth, and if you are like most people, the first time you are hooked up you'll become anxious. This means the first feedback you'll receive is negative, telling you that you're doing the wrong thing. If you are overly sensitive, this is another failure as far as you're concerned. So if biofeedback was in your plans talk to the teacher, trainer, or therapist and find out how he views his role. If he emphasizes that you and the equipment solve the problem and that his job is basically technical, look out. If he seems warm, responsive, interested, and describes himself as a facilitator to help you help yourself, you can have a little more confidence in this procedure.

With respect to more cognitively oriented procedures it will be important to select one, or to design the training, in such a way that you'll be able to experience some early success. The lower your level of self-esteem, the more you'll need the power of positive thinking but the less likely you'll be able to attain it, especially on your own.

Systematic desensitization should be chosen over implosion, particularly if you have suffered an actual breakdown in your ability to function in the past. But your best bet may be cognitive behavior modification rather than something like mental rehearsal because it will provide you with much-needed support.

What are your treatment goals?

Last, but by no means least, treatment design will depend a great deal on your goals. Too often people look for help without knowing what they want it for. You can end up spending weeks, months, or even years in trying to define a problem. Few of us can afford to walk into a store with an open pocketbook, casually gazing at whatever is in front of us and buying things that catch our fancy whether they are needed or not. Therapy without goals is no different.

The important thing to remember is that stress prevention implies a life-long program, since stressful situations will always be with us. So the program you choose must be practiced on a regular basis for the rest of your life. This requires a great deal of dedication, self-discipline, and motivation.

Autogenics, progressive relaxation, TM and exercise programs all lend themselves to this goal. Biofeedback can be used to reinforce training by providing evidence, through the feedback, that the procedures are in fact working. However, biofeedback alone is impractical since it is expensive and difficult to have the equipment handy when you need it.

In a similar way, hypnosis is also difficult to apply within a prevention situation on a regular basis. It would be nice if a post-hypnotic suggestion could be given that would last for the rest of our lives, either keeping us relaxed or giving us the discipline to practice some procedure. But this isn't possible, so it limits the use of hypnosis for every situation and individual. Because of these constraints, goals are very important in terms of defining and isolating the things you'll need for today and the future. For this reason we offer here some common goals and the treatments that apply for those specific situations.

1. I want to treat a specific physical symptom that occurs in a specific situation.

These problems are usually fairly easy to treat and respond rapidly to an intervention program. Since the focus is on physical symptoms, it will be easier for you to remain motivated and to believe in the procedure if it has a similar focus. There are procedures that can directly affect symptoms; however, for this to happen two things are necessary:

a) You'll need to increase your sensitivity to changes in muscle tension and other bodily functions. It is important to detect a problem early so that it doesn't reach such a painful point that you are incapable of concentrating on the treatment procedure.

b) In addition to increased sensitivity you must have some means of gaining control. Biofeedback could prove to be an excellent way to increase sensitivity and to gain control if you follow the directions that will be given in an upcoming chapter. There are also other procedures you might consider such as a mental rehearsal process (cognitive behavior modification would be used more for sensitizing you to attitudinal problems).

Progressive relaxation is another excellent procedure that can be used to gain control once you are sensitized. It is less expensive than biofeedback and easier to implement in the actual situation. Progressive relaxation also can be modified to emphasize certain muscle groups or to focus more intensely on affected areas. You'll find that mental rehearsal, as a sensitizer in combination with progressive relaxation, is often very effective.

2. I want to treat a specific physical problem that occurs under a variety of circumstances.

The fact that a symptom occurs in a great many situations and may or may not be stress-related is critical. If there is an obvious stress connection to a particular situation, then a procedure such as systematic desensitization or cognitive behavior modification could be used to lessen the ability of the situation to upset you.

In the absence of a stress connection, the best results are obtained through direct treatment of the symptoms. For migraine headaches the goal is to relax and thus cause a redistribution of blood flow to the peripheral blood vessels. Biofeedback of finger temperature has been a very successful procedure for accomplishing this. Autogenic training, with suggestions for the warming of fingers and hands being emphasized, as well as hypnotic suggestion, have also been found helpful with migraines.

In the case of other physical symptoms, especially those dealing with muscle pain, biofeedback would be a good choice. Pain seemingly unrelated to physiopathology has been found to be responsive to hypnotic suggestions. If the problem has to do with high blood pressure, then a procedure practiced on a regular basis would be used. Any of those in Part I could be equally effective, with your choice depending on your personality and particular needs and expectations.

3. I want to improve my ability to perform physically in a specific situation.

With this type of goal the primary concern is with controlling a variety of physical symptoms (muscle tension, perspiration, heart and breathing rate) that result from pressure and interfere with performance. It doesn't make sense to try to attack a whole group of symptoms, but rather to tackle them one at a time if there is a single cause.

When this is the case, and there is no desire to learn new ways of behaving or to develop new skills, systematic desensitization would be an effective aid. All that is required is to help you function at your normal level under pressure. This can be accomplished by reducing the ability of the particular situation to generate pressure and by increasing your self-confidence. Self-hypnosis as well as hypnosis could also be used.

The potential danger with hypnosis is that a hypnotist's suggestions could interfere with performance rather than facilitate it. If hypnosis is used, make sure the hypnotist knows the demands of the situation so he doesn't have you doing, or thinking about, things at inappropriate times.

4. I want to improve my ability to perform physically in a variety of situations and develop new skills.

This is a common goal of athletes, musicians, doctors, teachers—in fact, of most of us. Usually two factors are involved in accomplishing it. First, you must develop good control over physical arousal so that you can improve the overall consistency of your performance. This can be achieved by using any of the procedures in Part I. Second, for skill development, a mental rehearsal or cybernetics type of procedure could be used. If attitude is not a problem but behavior is, then either cognitive behavior modification or mental rehearsal would be effective.

The next series of goals have to do with alterations in emotional processes.

1. I want to prevent the apathy and depression that can occur as a function of continual pressure.

As with physical problems, a true prevention program will require the development of new habits and self-statements that become an automatic part of your life. For those of you who are not under a great deal of pressure at the present time and who have some past successes, practice in positive thinking can be effective when trouble comes.

If you can sit still and don't need a great deal of structure, TM should be considered since it is a very useful procedure when one wants to learn to develop a passive-reflective attention. This passive attitude can also be a very good way to break up negative cognitive symptoms, Benson's relaxation response is another useful procedure for this. On the other hand, both self-hypnosis and cognitive behavior modification are better suited to the treatment of problems than to their prevention.

2. I want to treat a specific problem that arises in a specific situation.

It is important to notice that with this goal performance improvement won't be an issue. Systematic desensitization would be a useful treatment in any situation where anxiety or fear is the major concern and actual performance is not. Implosion could be equally effective.

Situations where anxiety may be high but performance is not important would involve fears where there is no possibility of your assuming control. Fear of flying or a fear of cancer would be examples. Here there is nothing you can do or learn that will reduce the actual possibility of a plane crash or of your getting cancer.

Hypnosis, self-hypnosis, and cognitive behavior modification can all be used to treat fears. If the fear is due to some long-standing, underlying conflict hypnosis will lend itself to in-depth analysis of the problem. Self-hypnosis, and positive thinking can be used, but if the fear is intense then the self-control aspects of these procedures become a problem.

Carefully assess your own need for support and the intensity of your fear. The higher both of these are, the more difficult it will be to make progress. This is especially true since the only positive effect of this type of training is a reduction of your own fear. If you could also improve performance as a function of your training, then that fact alone would act to increase self-confidence. But since performance is not relevant it is more difficult.

3. I want to treat a general problem that I experience in a variety of situations.

The more intense the feelings of inadequacy (even though performance is good, and others see you as doing an acceptable job), the more long-term your program will be, and the more you will need external support from family, friends and trainers.

It is possible, however, to minimize these needs by narrowing your focus. In effect, all you have to do is reduce the demands you place on yourself by focusing on only one aspect of the problem. This will allow a procedure such as systematic desensitization or cognitive behavior modification to be effective.

If you find the inadequacy persisting and are unable to stick with one aspect of the problem, you'll need a consultation with a skilled professional. When you have a great deal of difficulty believing in your ability, it is usually because of some underlying conflict. Under these circumstances more traditional forms of psychoanalysis will be helpful.

4. I want to improve my mental performance.

If this is your goal, then the concern should be with controlling a variety of mental, perceptual, and emotional symptoms that develop as a function of stress. Cognitive behavior modification would be a treatment of choice because it focuses on both attitude change (making positive self-statements) and provides direction concerning more appropriate ways to deal with the situation behaviorally.

Self-hypnosis tends to be a little less helpful here because there is less outside support, and self-instructions tend to be more general pats on the back. This procedure, though, can be modified so more specific statements are given. This might be accomplished by using self-hypnosis, progressive relaxation, or even TM in combination with mental rehearsal procedures. The relaxation procedure is selected on the basis of other factors such as your attitude and needs. You should try to relax first and then rehearse specific behaviors that relate to successful performance.

As we have tried to emphasize, the most effective programs will employ multiple procedures or will be modified in such a way that both emotional and physical processes will be dealt with. Most of you will want to do the same kind of thing for yourselves. You may feel a little bit as you do when ordering a Chinese dinner. You get to select one from group A (physical) and one from group B (emotional).

In the next chapters we will detail specific procedures within their own particular focus, whether it be emotional, physical or a combination of the two. A great many of you will be able to design and implement your own programs without any difficulty at all. Others may need some brief guidance and assistance. And let's face it, self-control procedures are not for everyone. As you have looked at your own concerns, you may have decided that you would like some additional assistance. In the final chapter we have attempted to give you some guidelines to follow, as well as where to go for more help.

Part Two

HOW TO IMPROVE MENTAL CONTROL

3

Meditation

Meditation, in one form or another, has been with man for thousands of years, and because of this there are countless procedures we could mention. However, rather than trying to cover everything, which wouldn't be useful in the long run, we've limited our discussions to a select few procedures that have the most research behind them and are most readily available in the United States.

We have chosen to look at Transcendental Meditation (a yogi form of meditation); a meditative exercise that directs attention to breathing (a variation of both a Zen procedure and Benson's procedures); and also a physical exercise as a form of meditation.

Unfortunately, choosing the right meditative procedure can be a lot like selecting a foreign car—there are some sexy-looking models, but the service can be awful. With the following procedures you can at least get guidance. In addition, there is enough information available about them to provide you with the basis for developing any needed trust or confidence.

Transcendental Meditation

It is only fitting that the Magical Mystery Tour age of the Beatles should spawn an entirely different discipline for Westerners in the form of Transcendental Meditation. No other musical group since Joshua and his trumpets has had such an impact as these four men from Liverpool, and so it was appropriate that when they visited the mystical East they should bring back the venerable Maharishi Mahesh Yogi and his teachings of TM.

Suddenly the counter-culture with its questioning and rule-breaking ways had a banner to cling to. Although the 60s will be remembered more for the campus unrest over Viet Nam and black civil rights, it was within this context that TM made its dramatic entry into the mainstream of middle America.

TM held out the hope for inner peace and tranquility that neatly mixed the old with the new. The East had practiced meditation for centuries before the Western world caught up with its success. But suddenly the gurus and yogis were the new heroes, and millions flocked to have their problems washed away by the light of inner reason.

TM offered, and still does, the opportunity to get one's head together. It was that simple. One needed only between $125.00 and $200.00 * and about 40 minutes each day to learn to calm your inner being, reduce fatigue, and achieve a "higher level of consciousness." All that was required was that you be given minimal instructions, a special word, or *mantra*, selected for you, and the requirement that you practice regularly.

Scientific research showed that TM actually reduced

---

* Weekend and week-long retreats are available for additional fees.

physiological arousal. And it was this passive nature of TM that fit in nicely with the anti-establishment attitudes of the 60s.

A passive-reflective attention is at the base of almost every meditative procedure. In the case of TM it is a mantra; in the case of Benson's procedures it is a number; in the case of some Zen exercises it is breathing or the "one point." In all of these your attention is never forced, but rather you allow yourself to perceive the desired object or focus. If your mind wanders you simply reflect the wandering in a passive way and let yourself return to the mantra. For the counter-culture of the 60s this was a pleasant change from the high-drive, intense, controlling, active attention that had been at the base of the anti-war movement and social unrest.

Passive attention was important, but it alone would not have been enough. Probably the single most important event responsible for TM's popularity was a project conducted by Wallace and Benson, two researchers on the faculty at Harvard University. They were able to demonstrate that practice in TM was associated with reduction in respiration rate, heart rate, and blood pressure. They also found that there was a rapid breakdown of lactate in the blood. It was believed that lactate build-up was one major factor in the development of fatigue.

There were also many subjective changes. Individuals reported feeling better, happier, and more involved. They experienced less upset and anxiety while having more energy and a greater willingness to look at old things with a new perspective.

The basic findings of Wallace and Benson have been substantiated by others, and today TM is a useful procedure for reducing general levels of arousal. If it is employed on a regular basis (twice a day for 20 minutes at a time), for the rest of your life, it can minimize the likelihood of your developing those chronic emotional and physical problems associated with stress.

The enthusiasm of people for what they have found in TM needs to be tempered at times. There can be a tendency to attribute too much to it. Recent research on the brain has attempted to identify specific functions associated with particular areas. Some of the findings have indicated that the two hemispheres of the brain may be specialized for different functions. The right side (in most right-handed people) seems to be used for intuition and feeling. It is also on this side that irrational faith would be located. The left side, however, tends to be more logical and sequential and also specialized for language functions and reason.

Meditators have been quick to propose the idea that the Western world is dominated by the left side of the brain. The tendency has been to suggest that meditation strengthens the right side.

In truth, there is no sound evidence to suggest that TM, or any other meditative procedure, acts on a particular side of the brain. What can be said is that meditation and passive attention will lead to general reductions in arousal no matter what procedure is used. There are brain wave changes associated with the relaxation, as well as changes in respiration rate, but any stress reduction procedure will cause the same general changes in physiology. The impact of the changes, the interpretation and meaning that you apply, will depend on your own understanding of the procedures and your beliefs.

TM has been effective in reducing stress in millions of people. Nancy is a case in point. Her father was a successful businessman residing in a wealthy Chicago suburb. The middle child, with an older and younger brother, Nancy always felt the need to overachieve in what was a very competitive household. Foregoing sports at an early age, she channeled her energies into her school work and attained high grades and the promise for future scholastic honors. The fact that she was a better student than either of her brothers tended to add impetus to her continually expanding goals.

By the time Nancy entered college, there was no question in her mind that medicine (psychiatry in particular) would be stimulating and challenging enough for her considerable intellectual abilities. Nancy's need to achieve and her competitiveness had gotten her involved in a number of controversial issues. She had been an early advocate of women's rights, and it was not surprising that she would choose a career so dominated by men.

She found the inner workings of the mind fascinating and this provided fertile ground for her to test her own theories. The choice of a profession that caused her to come face to face with other people's concerns and problems, and to solve them when they couldn't, was mute testimony to her own need for power and control.

Upon her graduation, with honors, from a large mid-western university, Nancy took time to travel extensively through Europe. It was at this point in her life that she met her husband, an artist who had gained success in his own right. The marriage was ideal, with each respecting the other's career goals and the need for space to attain further achievements. In time they decided to move to New York City, feeling that this would be advantageous to both of their careers.

Nancy set up her practice and enjoyed a rather remarkable following. By now her family included a husband, a small girl and boy, and two cats. At 35 she had achieved much and had a great deal to show for her perseverence and dedication.

Her patients were predominately corporate executives

whose major problems were those associated with the stresses of a great need to achieve. For the most part they were similar to Nancy in their drives for excellence and control. Because their own drive for success had gotten out of control they came to her with addiction problems, hypertension, guilt, and anxiety.

It was during the treatment of these patients that Nancy became sensitized to some of her own needs and problems. She recognized within herself the same drive for perfection; the tendency to try to be all things to all people. It was a conflict that found her wanting to be a good therapist, a good mother, and a good wife. Hers was not the problem of resentment since she loved her busy life—rather, it was over-commitment. With each year her life became more complicated as she added responsibility to responsibility without relinquishing any.

Something was bound to give under the strain of her professional life. Unfortunately, the part of her that began to suffer was her personal life. Nancy knew that by the time she came home from the office she was drained and had little energy left to spend on her family and husband. To make matters worse, sexual relations, which were an important part of her marriage, had been reduced to almost nothing. She was simply too tired.

When her relationship with her husband began to waver and she saw that she was losing control of her children, Nancy began to direct her attention to these conflicts in her own life. She recognized that she had to do something to preserve what had been a very stable family situation.

Throughout her life Nancy had been in control of her own destiny, and she was not about to relinquish that part of her personality. Rather than going to a professional for help, Nancy set out to find the solution to her own problems.

Her high level of achievement and her identification with many of the attitudes of the 60s had brought her into contact with Eastern as well as Western thought. She realized that in the business world specifically, and in Western society as a whole, the rewards were for achievement and drive, two characteristics she had in abundance. She recognized that like her patients she didn't know how to relax. She had neglected that aspect of her education but now saw a need to learn to take a more passive, easygoing attitude.

Nancy began reading the TM literature and the studies regarding its effectiveness as a stress reducer. After a few weeks she became convinced that TM could be used to achieve the results she wanted. She took part in four training sessions and reorganized her schedule in order to practice meditation each day after work. (Although two sessions are recommended, Nancy found one was sufficient for her needs—she wasn't ready to become *that* passive).

The changes Nancy noticed were startling. She found herself being replenished during these times when she shut her mind off to the rest of the world. Previously she came home tired, having listened to the problems of patients all day, being actively involved and drained by the continual flow of input, and at times bringing her work home with her. Nancy now saw that meditation was an avenue to clear away this over-loading.

She was able, in essence, to empty her head and thus feel rejuvenated. Her increased energy and capacity to relax made her more than able to attend to her family for the remaining four or five hours of the day, without taking away anything from her physically or emotionally. For Nancy, TM supplied the little extra needed to manage successfully both her personal and professional life.

Many of us find ourselves in similar situations. We are

overcommitted and overinvolved. We don't have a specific problem to focus on; instead we simply need to learn to relax and to conserve energy. TM is especially adapted to those situations.

For Nancy it was easy to place faith in TM because she reorganized and accepted the importance of a passive attitude. Some of us have more difficulty accepting that concept. An equally important factor is the high level of self-esteem and discipline required to maintain regular practice in the absence of outside support from a therapist or trainer. Had Nancy been less self-motivated, or had she doubted her own ability to institute a program and to solve her own problem, TM might not have been so useful.

Some of the factors that get in the way of using TM include the following: 1) an inability to accept and develop a passive attitude; 2) an inability to sit still or to find the time to set aside 20 minutes for regular practice; 3) the need to deal actively and immediately with a situation.

If your problem is one that demands involvement and does not allow you to take 20 minutes out to meditate, TM may be difficult to apply. Finally, many people need more support than one receives in the four initial training sessions. True, there are TM groups and TM retreats you can go on. These activities are for groups and usually require a certain amount of willingness, on your part, to expose yourself to others. Often this is difficult for people to do, especially when they perceive the meditative experience as a very private one.

If you feel that TM can offer you something that other procedures can't, additional information is available at TM centers in most large cities. Just consult the yellow and white pages under TM and under meditation. Introductory lectures are typically free, since they provide a sales opportunity for trainers who derive at least part of their income from this source. Check with community agencies, churches, and schools to see if any lectures are planned in your area.

The Relaxation Response

Another form of the physical path to stress reduction is set forth in Herbert Benson's book, *The Relaxation Response*. The actual procedures presented by Benson combine aspects of TM with a focus on breathing that is common to many Zen meditative procedures.

Benson was one of the authors of the study that helped to launch TM. He continued his research and developed his own notions concerning relaxation. What you may find interesting is that Wallace, his co-author, went on to become the president of Maharishi International University.

In *The Relaxation Response,* Benson maintains that relaxation and the reduction of arousal that individuals experience in TM or other meditative procedures is the result of stimulating an innate human response. Research on both humans and animals has indicated that there are specific centers of the brain that when stimulated generate arousal. From this Benson concluded that there were also centers for relaxation.

It is Benson's contention that the relaxation response (alteration in heart rate, brain-wave activity, and respiration) is elicited by any number of procedures which encompass the following four factors: 1) The procedures must be practiced on a regular basis. Apparently a lack of activity results in some reduction in our ability to elicit the response. 2) The individual should sit quietly. A position such as sitting is suggested because those positions that are too relaxing (lying down) result in the individual's falling asleep. There is nothing wrong with falling asleep, but it is not meditation, and sleep does not lead to the rapid recovery from fatigue. 3) Outside noises and visual interference should be reduced to a minimum in order to avoid distractions. 4) The individual must pick a simple stimulus to attend to. A TM mantra is a simple stimulus, the number "one" is a simple stimulus, as are short prayers or any number of things. Attention should be passive as opposed to active.

Benson's notions came into conflict with those of TM at several critical points. For him the mysticism of an Eastern doctrine was unimportant if the basis for the procedure was sound. For this reason the word *one* could be substituted for a secret mantra. In TM it is emphasized that the mantra is secret because it is supposed to be a meaningless sound to facilitate passive attention. For Benson any simple stimulus or word, repeated over and over again, would quickly lose meaning.

Another difference between TM and Benson's procedure is that in TM attention is not called to anything other than the mantra and then only in a passive way. In Benson's procedures attention is directed to breathing by connecting it to the mantra. All you have to do is count *one* to yourself on each breath. This little additional bit of structure can serve to direct the attention in certain ways increasing the tendency to control the breathing to direct relaxation instead of just letting it happen. If successful, then relaxation may occur more rapidly than it would with TM. Some people however, particuarly those with respiratory problems or whose breathing is affected by stress, may be upset by this focus rather than relaxed.

Benson's procedure, like TM, is useful for the prevention of chronic problems and for achieving a general lowering of arousal. The practice of passive concentration is also an excellent way to rid yourself of negative thoughts. The better you get at it the easier it is to put frightening things out of your mind.

As with TM, this particular procedure does not translate readily to those situations where you want to gain control under pressure. The hope here is that a brief amount of time (20 minutes) will allow you to pull yourself together and function better.

To look at the importance of being able to attend passively to fears, as well as seeing the logic and reason behind a specific procedure, consider the case of Karen. Benson's procedure was chosen because it emphasized breathing, which was important in Karen's case. In addition, Karen needed the little bit of extra purpose that went along with focusing on breathing since she had something to accomplish.

Karen's problem had begun some five years before she started treatment. Like many people she had always been somewhat anxious whenever she had to go to the doctor, fearing both the procedure and also what might be discovered. There was just something uncomfortable about being exposed and examined.

Karen had come from a middle-class family who held fairly conventional values. She was sensitive and tended to see authority figures, and doctors in particular, as superior beings. She had started dating when she was 14, and by the time she was 16 she had a steady boyfriend. Up until the time she went away to college she always responded to the admonition not to engage in sexual behavior. However, in college things began to change.

Karen was away from home for the first time and found herself among girls from all over the country. Sexual relations were talked about openly in the dorm and seemed to be a natural part of life. For Karen this was difficult to accept, and what made it more disturbing was that her boyfriend, though initially patient and understanding, was putting more and more pressure on her and had even begun dating other girls.

She did her best to convince herself that her parents' ideas were old fashioned and finally succeeded to the point of going to a local clinic to obtain some birth-control pills. The waiting room was crowded, and Karen began to get upset. As she sat there she began to feel as though everyone in the room knew what she had come for. She began having second thoughts, felt guilty about what she was doing, and probably would have walked out if the nurse hadn't chosen that time to come out and ask her to follow her to an examination room.

The nurse opened the door to the room and motioned for Karen to step inside. Karen was handed a hospital gown and was told to take off her clothes. The nurse then informed her that the doctor would be along in minute and proceded to walk out of the room.

Through all of this the busy nurse failed to notice the anxiety etched on Karen's face. As she left, Karen took her first good look at the room and her heart sank. There stood the examination table, complete with stirrups, and Karen recalled every story she had ever heard about dirty old doctors and young girls. She was so shaken that she just stood there fighting back the tears and unable to run out of the clinic.

About this time the nurse returned and noticing that Karen had not yet taken off her clothes shouted at her: "I thought I told you to get undressed! Hurry up!" With that, the nurse stormed out of the room.

Meekly Karen took off her clothes and lay on the table, feeling sick to her stomach and recalling all of the should's and should not's her parents had told her. Soon the doctor came in.

His manner was cold and impersonal. "I need to take some blood ... make a fist ... this won't hurt." Like the nurse, the doctor seemed too busy to pay attention to the upset condition of a young girl. He didn't see the tears, he didn't notice the breathing. As he began the vaginal exam he did notice that Karen was a little tight and responded by saying, "Just relax; you're too tight; relax!"

When Karen began therapy she was still suffering from the exam. She had long since broken up with her old boyfriend, was now married, and expecting her first child. Part of her problem was that her fear was so great she was avoiding going to the doctor. She had gone a couple of times and the anxiety was almost more than she could handle. She found herself tightening up so much that the exam was very painful. A side effect to this was that Karen anticipated problems with the delivery if she could not learn to relax.

Benson's procedure was ideal for Karen for two reasons. First, she needed to break away from all the anxious thoughts that were developing. The practice of passive concentration was particularly helpful for this. Additionally, since Karen had begun classes in natural childbirth, she was learning various breathing techniques. It was easy for her to transfer what she was being taught in both situations, allowing her to focus on breathing. This was something positive to attend to that was associated with relaxation, responding in a way that would help both her and the expected baby.

She was able to relax enough to considerably lessen the pain she experienced during check-ups and found that she was able to enjoy her pregnancy far more than was previously the case.

The use of a breathing procedure to reduce pain and the use of passive concentration to stop arousing anxiety-provoking stimuli are two important ways that Benson's procedure can be used. TM can accomplish similar things, but the addition of breathing provides a fairly strong physical focus for some people, making it far easier to get away from anxiety than is possible from a simple mantra. So if you worry a great deal it may be easier to use the breathing procedure.

Fear of physicians and dentists is all too common. How many times have you found yourself sitting in the dentist's chair with your hands tightly clenched. Every muscle in your arms, back, and shoulders is rigid, and you are locked in on the sound of the drill. The next time that happens to you you might just try TM or a breathing meditation.

We mentioned briefly that the focus on breathing could sometimes help individuals to *get out* of their heads and that this was a potential advantage of this procedure over TM. For many people there is such a high level of activity, as well as a need for constant mental and physical activity, that it is virtually impossible to sit still. This is true for young children and for many of us who have a high need to achieve. The mere thought of sitting quietly for 20 minutes to meditate may generate more anxiety than any problem ever could.

Many people have recognized this, and it is one of the reasons that a great number of meditative exercises involve physical activity. In our own society we have seen a great interest in jogging, tennis, swimming, and other aerobic exercises, with cardiologists advocating these types of physical activity as a means of increasing muscle tone and reducing stress. But not everyone is a prime candidate for regular, strenuous workouts—Hank provides a perfect example.

In many ways Hank was the typical businessman, even to the point of having his first heart attack when he was 45 years old. Fairly athletic throughout high school and college, with letters in both football and baseball when he graduated, Hank was recruited by a large corporation for a management position. He advanced rapidly by pushing himself and other people, showing little patience for what he perceived to be incompetence. Hank was a difficult man to work for, and many failed to last on his "team."

At home Hank was equally difficult in the way he controlled the people around himself, but the major problem in his regimented life was that his own physical activity had dropped off to an occasional round of golf and other weekend sports. For the most part he had become the TV spectator.

To Hank, relaxing was watching a sports event with a drink in one hand and something to munch in his other hand. However, even when relaxing Hank was in constant motion. If he wasn't lifting something to his mouth, he was reaching for a paper, changing the channels on the TV, or making one of his frequent trips to the bathroom.

During these hours Hank expected his wife and children to leave him alone. He thought of himself as king of his castle and insisted that his wishes be respected. But no matter how hard he tried Hank could never truly unwind and enjoy these private moments.

Hank had been warned by the company doctor that he suffered from high blood pressure and that he should try to lose weight and stop smoking. Each time he saw the doctor Hank accepted the advice and said, "sure."

Hank never really tried to follow the doctor's orders. He was stubborn and persistant, believing that sometimes the hard way was the only way and that one should continue until successful. He had accomplished things with this approach and wasn't about to let a doctor take over his life.

However, life changed dramatically for Hank when he

suffered a heart attack. He had never been incapacitated before and found it all but impossible to lay quietly on his back in the hospital. He finally promised the doctor he would change his life if he would just let him go home.

The results were startling. He went on a diet and lost 10 pounds almost overnight. He also quit smoking and started to exercise—at least he started doing what he considered to be exercise. He jogged every morning, but as soon as this activity became routine, Hank began using the time while running to plan out the day's events. He couldn't break away from work even while running, and the stress stayed with him.

Hank's positive results were short-lived. His weight started to creep back up, and his wife pestered him about it. Annoyed with himself and everyone around him, Hank would get angry at his wife, telling her to mind her own business. She became concerned because she knew her nagging was only stressing him more. She was damned if she said something and damned if she didn't. Finally, to get out of the house and partially appease his wife, Hank took up gold again . . . with a vengeance.

He still had heavy responsibilities at work, but he would dash home to play immediately after his business day. He'd jump into a change of clothes, climb into his golf cart, and take off for a solo trip around the course. He would do his best to cram 18 holes into two hours before sunset, and would even play two balls—to compete with himself. One day about two years after the first heart attack Hank failed to come home—he had died on the golf course of a second heart attack.

Hank would never have been able to get involved in any program that restricted his activity—he needed to be active. He also needed to be in control of his own program. Jogging, although a fine exercise for many people, simply gave Hank the opportunity to think about his problems. He unfortunately was unable to use it to get out of his head and into the experience.

Although we will never know for sure, Hank probably would have been much better off engaging in some physical activity that was complicated enough to keep him mentally busy. The right activity would have had to demand his total attention and concentration while also being non-competitive. Thus he would have been better off practicing in isolation or with a teacher rather than in a group situation. Some yogic exercises or Tai Chi would have met those requirements.

The next case has a happier ending. It illustrates the application of an effective physical program to reduce stress.

Ken was 43 years old, a high school principal who had been in an administrative position for the past 15 years. Ken, his wife, and their three children had lived in the same house for the past 10 years, ever since Ken had been promoted from vice-principal to principal. In their city of about 150,000 people, Ken and his family had developed roots and a sense of community involvement. He knew most of the business and community leaders, and his children were firmly ensconced in school, with the eldest even thinking about attending a local university rather than leaving his home town.

Ken's problem was not too dissimilar from that of many of the younger corporate executives that he knew. In fact, he would often talk to them about the frustrations they seemed to share. Earning $40,000 per year, with good benefits and job security, Ken had achieved a reasonable amount of success. But he saw that he couldn't expect to go any higher in his profession, and at 43 he was already looking forward to retirement. He knew how to handle his job as principal and no longer enjoyed the challenge that was once present. He was not really interested in a political position or in one that removed him from working with people, and the position of school superintendent was the last thing he wanted.

His corporate friends empathized with his plight but offered no solutions. They too experienced similar frustration, being close to the top of their organizations with 15 to 20 years to go before retirement. Unfortunately, the people whose positions they would occupy were also years away from retirement. Most had become used to their level of income and were unwilling to risk what they had by moving to a new job elsewhere or totally changing careers in mid-stream.

He found himself building up a great deal of resentment and frustration, found himself losing his temper over little things and blamed his wife and family for the trapped feeling he was experiencing. His relationships with the faculty began suffering for similar reasons. He had little tolerance for their concerns, especially when they seemed to be repeats of earlier problems. He had gone full circle with respect to the number of different approaches used to deal with student and faculty problems. He had introduced more structure when that seemed like the answer, and when the demand was for independence he had adapted easily. But the shifts back and forth became predictable, causing Ken to become tired of the predictability of it all.

As Ken became more frustrated and less involved, his activity level decreased both at work and at home. He found himself drained, with little or no energy left to enjoy things he had once looked to for release. At first he attributed it to the fact that he was over 40, but then he noticed that others his age didn't seem to have the same dilemma. When Ken went to his family physician for a physical he mentioned the feelings that he was having and the doctor suggested that he consider therapy as a way out of the abyss he was falling into.

In talking to Ken it became clear that one of his problems was that he was over-idealistic. His inactivity found him perpetually dreaming of better days and what could have been. Instead of thinking about positive things and solving real problems, Ken alternated between his fantasies and the hopelessness of his situation.

Ken's tendency to become trapped in his own thoughts and his low level of energy made it clear that he should get involved in an active physical program. Since depression can lead to inactivity and then back to more depression in a vicious cycle, reinvolvement in physical activities will tend to break the pattern and lift the depression.

Ken began a daily exercise regimen, and in a matter of weeks he found that his energy had returned, along with some of his former enthusiasm. Unlike some of his business friends he did not have to move up to feel successful although he did need something to get involved in. In addition to the swimming and yoga exercises that had been prescribed, it was also suggested that Ken and his wife consider participating in a marriage encounter weekend.

Ken was insightful enough to recognize what his own frustration had been doing to his marriage. He loved his wife and consented to give the counseling a try. The results were most rewarding. The two of them were able to deal with their feelings as well as find new areas of mutual interest to conquer. They both learned massage and began to practice on each other, deriving great pleasure from what they now were able to add to their relationship. Instead of having his frustrations build when he came home, Ken was able to let himself go while directing his attention to the feelings and sensations created by his wife's now-skilled hands.

For Ken and his wife the results were similar to those one

might expect from TM. The feelings generated by their partners served as the mantra breaking them out of negative thoughts and allowing them to unwind. Ken's energy returned, his marriage improved, and his work became more satisfying than it had been for many years.

Once again we find ourselves emphasizing passive attention because it is the key to successful meditation. The ability to be aware of what is going on in your body, to reflect the fact that your heart is beating rapidly, and to react passively to that fact is what breaks the panic and the chronic high levels of arousal associated with stress.

Adopting a passive response is not difficult to understand. For example, what if you were watching a television program you really wanted to see and one of your children came home and started jumping around to get your attention? You could react in two ways: In a very passive approach you'd say, "That's nice," and continue with the program. You would have reflected on what went on and then have allowed yourself to concentrate on what you were interested in. You could have also responded by getting annoyed and shouting at your child, thus causing stress where there needn't be any and also changing your focus away from something you were intently watching.

By practicing meditation and passively attending to a mantra or your breathing, you can learn to be relaxed under most situations. You can break the self-defeating spiral that is associated with stress, but you must practice to learn to do so. You don't usually learn to swim by jumping in the deep end. To attempt to learn to meditate when you were highly anxious would be comparable to that.

Dr. Benson and many others have identified factors that make it easier to learn to meditate. First, practice regularly. Second, practice in a quiet setting where you can reduce the number of potential distractions, especially the number of anxiety-related factors. If your children are part of the problem don't try to meditate when they are around, within hearing distance, or likely to come home. If even the smallest thought about their interfering creeps in, it will be awfully difficult to treat it passively, especially in the beginning.

The final suggestion is to find some neutral stimulus to return your attention to in order to clear your mind and gently break away from anxiety-inducing distractions. This is what is behind the type of meditation we will be presenting. It is also important to point out what is missing.

TM offers you several different things. First, there is a ceremony involved with TM. You are interviewed by a teacher and are provided with a mantra to meditate on. The mantra is a meaningless sound, which you are told to keep secret. For some people this ceremony is important. Next, TM offers you human contact and support in the form of the teacher and other meditators. This, too, can be a major factor, especially in helping you to maintain motivation and build confidence. You need both of those supports, although how you get them isn't important. If you can provide your own, you will be able to save the meditation fee.

The fee brings up another factor that is related to confidence. We live in such a money-oriented society that it is sometimes difficult for people to place confidence in something that they don't pay for. Paying a fee may make you feel you are buying something special and help motivate you to practice. (After all, you can't let the money go to waste.)

Money could be a very important motivator for you, but you don't have to spend it on someone else. Why don't you set aside the money you would spend on training for something special that you really want. Then pay yourself that money for practicing the procedures and developing self-control. If you don't earn the money then spend it on a trainer.

Step I

Identify a quiet place and time. It is helpful to have the security of knowing you will not be interrupted and that your time is your own. Many people find early morning, before dinner, or just before going to bed to be the best times. Housewives often use the time immediately after everyone leaves in the morning. Perhaps you are lucky enough to have someone who will *happily* run interference and give you the space and time you'll need.

Step II

The first few times you meditate just spend about five minutes. Gradually (at your own speed), work up to 20 minutes once or twice a day. There is little value for most people in going beyond that amount of practice. You won't learn any faster by practicing more, and you run the risk of creating stress by not getting your daily work done.

Step III

Get into a sitting position that isn't so comfortable that you'll fall asleep. Make sure that anything such as dangling jewelry or contact lenses are removed so that they don't disturb you.

Step IV

Begin attending to your breathing, but don't try to control it. As you inhale, silently count *ooooone*. As you exhale count *twoooo*. It's all right if your mind wanders and you forget to count. Simply reflect the distraction,

"Oh, my mind wandered," and come back to the counting. At first the more your mind wanders the better off you are because each time it does you get to practice passive reflection. Counting for each breath and reflecting distractions is all you need do.

Notice that you do not *will* anything to happen. Your breathing will slow and relaxation will take place automatically. If you become aware of the process, simply reflect it like everything else: "Oh, my breathing slowed—back to counting." Even if distractions pile one on top of another, don't get into a fight for control.

Think of each distraction as an opportunity for more practice. Some people like to modify the breathing exercise slightly, and you can experiment to find what is best for you. The counting serves the same purpose as a mantra, and variations might include:

1. Counting "one" on each inhalation and not counting exhalations.
2. Counting inhalations and not counting exhalations but counting up to "two" (e.g. inhale "one," exhale, inhale "two," exhale, inhale "one," exhale).
3. Counting as follows: Inhale "one," exhale "two," inhale "three," exhale "four." Then start over again at "one."

4

Autogenic Training

Autogenic training is another of the stress-reduction procedures that focuses on changing physical feelings. Like TM and other meditative procedures, it requires you to learn a passive type of attention, and regular practice of the procedures can lead to reductions in arousal and anxiety. There are, however, some large differences between autogenics and other procedures that determine to whom the procedure can be applied and under what circumstances.

Autogenic training procedures were developed in the 1920s by two German physicians, Johannes Schultz and Wolfgang Luthe. These men had been using a variety of hypnotic techniques to reduce the stress and anxiety experienced by many of their patients. One of the things they noticed in their practice was that, independent of the method of induction, when relaxation occurred several identical changes developed in each individual.

In response to their observations they developed a rigid set of orderly, step-by-step procedures that were designed to develop feelings of relaxation quickly and efficiently. The procedures focused directly on changing physiological processes, such as heart rate and breathing. Convinced that by force of will alone individuals could change their bodily processes, they developed a set of formulae to be used to develop specific sensations.

This concept of "willing" your body to do something was an illusion. In practice what has to happen is that you must develop a passive attention. Take the first formula, "My right arm is heavy." In autogenic training you repeat this to yourself for a few seconds at a time, and eventually the feelings of heaviness develop. If you try to force the feeling you become aroused instead of relaxed, and your body fights with your mind for control. The inner dialogue between the two goes on as you find yourself checking to see if sensations are developing. Then when they don't you try to cope with the discouragement, only to find yourself more aroused and with a lessened degree of confidence.

Although it is an illusion, the concept of willing your body to do something is important. In reality, when practicing the formulae you do learn to reflect passively what happens so that the formulae become similar to a mantra, and relaxation thus natually occurs. For some people the notion of control and willing things to happen is easier than focusing on a mantra.

The autogenic procedures are practiced routinely twice a day. Each practice session involves two to four periods of passive concentration that last for 30 to 90 seconds. The idea is to learn to induce relaxation very quickly. Instead of requiring 20 minutes to meditate, you should be able to learn to calm yourself in a few seconds.

Most people require about six months of regular training in order to be able to induce all six of the feelings encompassed by the formulae. These include: 1) heaviness in arms and legs; 2) warmth in arms and legs; 3) cardiac control and regulation; 4) control of respiration; 5) warmth in the solar plexus; and 6) coolness in the forehead.

This highly structured approach to relaxation, the concept of willing your body to relax, and a very rapid induction of relaxation are the three critical differences between autogenics and other procedures. Since there is a direct attempt to control physiology, and because of its rigid structure, autogenics is often used by individuals who feel they should overcome and challenge adversity.

In addition, the procedure has particular application to athletic performance since individuals are not required to sit still for such a long period of time. Obviously sitting can be very difficult for many physically oriented people. Another reason for its practicality is that autogenics can be used to develop feelings of relaxation rapidly; thus they can be practiced just before and even during a performance. Finally, learning autogenic procedures requires dedication and practice. Change is gradual and, as mentioned, the average person takes about six months to complete the program. Even learning to develop heaviness in the right arm (the first task) may take as long as a week or two of regular practice.

Autogenic training does require a great deal of motivation and patience. For many this makes it a difficult procedure to employ. This is particularly true if you don't have six months to prepare for an anticipated situation. This motivational problem, however, can be overcome when autogenic training is used as an adjunct to a regular on-going therapy relationship. Under these circumstances the therapist provides continued encouragement and support, keeping you involved long enough to learn.

The cost of learning autogenic procedures, within the context of therapy, would probably range between $1,200 and $3,600. They can be self-taught, however, and are presented in this book. There are some warnings to be considered, particularly if you are older and/or suffer from some chronic physical or emotional problems. Under these conditions some professional supervision is required. A compromise approach many people have been able to use successfully is to organize a group. The procedures, because they are short, lend themselves nicely to group practice, thus serving to further motivate and reinforce each of the members.

For our purposes here, the following examples tend to show some of the benefits of applying autogenics to particular situations. In an upcoming chapter we present an example of the use of autogenic procedures in combination with mental rehearsal on a group of young AAU divers. For additional information read *Autogenic Training* (Grune and Stratton) by Schultz and Luthe.

Sam's story is our first example. Although always active in athletics, he had never achieved much success or recognition for his efforts. It wasn't that he didn't try; it was just that his accomplishments were never outstanding. The coach always pointed him out as an example of the right attitude, the one who always worked hard—but he seldom put Sam in the game. Rather than being put off or discouraged, Sam decided to try out for the swimming team during his sophomore year in college. He enjoyed diving in particular and made the team. Then it looked as if history was going to repeat itself. Although the team started with six divers, they soon had only three who continued to work out: the two who would be participating in each meet and Sam, who true to form kept plugging away.

That year the only diving he did was in practice and in the final conference meet. He was able to compete in the conference preliminaries because teams were not limited to the number of divers they could enter. For Sam it was an opportunity to test his skills, and although he performed adequately, he did not distinguish himself.

At the beginning of his junior year Sam was exposed (with the rest of his psychology class) to autogenic training. As a learning experiment the class was asked to apply the procedures to some aspect of their lives. Sam decided to direct his efforts to his diving. Fortunately, the support of both class and professor were impetus enough for him to feel confident in applying the procedure.

In many ways autogenics was the perfect procedure for the situation. During the course of a meet Sam knew that he had to be able to relax at various times. Since the procedures were so quick it was possible to utilize them either just before he got on the board to dive or as soon as he came to attention on the board. Most divers spend a few minutes in concentration just before each dive so that Sam's use of the procedures tended to fit right in to what his teammates were doing.

There were also other factors that convinced Sam of the practicality and ultimate benefits of the procedures. He knew that, like most other people, he responded to pressure with slight increases in muscle tension, and it was this physical reaction that could be critical in his diving. Sam would be twisting and somersaulting in the air; so the ability to have free movement of his neck, head, and shoulders was essential. If he could bend his head forward freely he would get the rotation needed in order to somersault and complete the dive. If he could not bend it (which often happens under intense pressure or when a diver is frightened), he would not be able to get all the way around and would consequently lose points on the dive. The margin for error was very small. On a given dive Sam might have less than 1/50th of a second in which to decide to open up for his entry into the water.

Sam started practicing autogenics in September for a season that ran from the middle of December to the middle of March. He found that he was able to listen as the referee announced his dive. He would then climb on the board and come to attention. It was at this point that he would take 30 seconds to repeat his formulae. Only when he had completed the phrases would be begin the approach for his dive.

Several things happened as a function of this training. First, . the consistency of Sam's performance improved dramatically. As his level of tension came more under control, so did his ability to time the execution and opening of his dive. Next, he won the conference diving championship. This occurred not just because of the improved consistency in performance but because his training fit his needs so nicely. Just as competition creates pressure, so does the thought of learning a new dive. In practice Sam found that he was less anxious. The result was that he learned five times the number of new dives his teammates learned. His lowered anxiety meant fewer mistakes when learning, so he experienced less pain from awkward landings. Since he wasn't getting hurt, it became easy to try new things.

Sam's case is not unique, and a similar application to a group of young divers will be discussed later. However, there are other areas where autogenic training can be very useful. In fact, almost any situation that requires you to make a decision or perform under pressure would provide an ideal testing ground.

Diane, a 30-year-old mother of two very active children, is proof of this. On good days she would describe her children as enthusiastic, interested, and playful. On bad days (which are all too frequent) they are seen as possessed, driven, incorrigible monsters who race through the house disrupting anything and anyone who gets in their way— including Diane.

By the tender age of five the eldest, Todd, had already

broken out a front window, knocked a hole in the dining room wall, colored the upholstery on the furniture, broken his nose flipping on the couch, made several trips to the emergency room for asthmatic reactions, and in general entertained and terrorized everyone within a four-block radius. Jay, the two-year-old, took advantage of every disturbance and diversion to wander off to forbidden and dangerous areas.

Throughout these taxing times Diane's husband was generously supportive whenever possible and tended to marvel at his wife's stamina, much like the man in the TV commercial who states that his wife can do it all, take care of the kids, clean the house, make dinner, and do all of this even with a cold—"My wife, I think I'll keep her." Diane did manage but began to feel the stress and strain wearing away at her.

It was nothing new—she had always had problems with time pressure. In school Diane could take a test and get an "A" every time, provided she knew she would be given all of the time she needed. If someone were to stick a clock or deadline in front of her, however, she would panic. Her mind would start racing, and all knowledge of the subject matter would vanish. This same thing occurred during the brief time Diane worked as a secretary. She could easily type 60 words per minute; but let someone come up behind her and look as if they were waiting for something, and suddenly 60 words per minute became six, and even some of those were misspelled.

Being somewhat extroverted and expressive, Diane was never one to cover her feelings in these situations. As things would begin to crumble she would get upset, angry, and had been known to yell, "If it weren't for you this wouldn't have happened." Then her anger would turn into embarrassment and feelings of self-recrimination.

It was because of this difficulty with pressure and

deadlines, that Diane did not go on for graduate work after college. She even quit her job as a secretary as quickly as she could for similar reasons. Now she finds herself in an equally harrowing situation from which there seems to be no escape.

"Mom, I want lunch." "Mom, take me to my friend's house." "Honey, don't forget to call the plumber." There were times when Diane felt that she might be going crazy. She described it as if there were a spring inside her compressed as tight as it could possibly be and ready to break loose. Sometimes she felt out of control and just wanted to scream.

Diane was capable of dealing with pressure. The fact that when she wasn't under time pressure she could answer test questions, type 60 words per minute, and care for her family indicated she had the ability to function effectively. Her downfall came when she let the demands confuse and disorganize her. By becoming worried about the pressure, she overloaded herself and damaged her ability to attend to each task.

It was because of this that a procedure such as autogenic training was used, since it allowed Diane to regain control quickly. Her problem was in dealing with *any* situation where time was a factor. Had it been more specific, some other procedure might have accomplished the same results in a shorter period of time. But as it was, once she learned the autogenic procedures, Diane found she could use them to reduce her rising anxiety quickly when she began to feel pushed and overloaded. The brief respite the exercise gave her allowed Diane to attend and make decisions far more effectively.

According to Schultz and Luthe there are several factors to keep in mind if you plan on practicing autogenic training.

1. Limit the use of the formulae to 30-90 seconds at a

time. This is especially important if your goal is to learn to relax very quickly.

2. Stay with the structure and order of suggestions. It is important to build a routine, and autogenics allows you to accomplish this.

3. Repeat the formula in an active way: "My right arm is heavy." But react passively and reflect whatever happens in a matter-of-fact way. Thus you might say, "My right arm is heavy," and at that time find your mind wandering and the thought, "No, it's not," entering consciousness. Reflect, "My mind wandered," and return to the formula, "My right arm is heavy." You might find it easier to concentrate if you close your eyes during the exercise.

4. If you have a history of heart problems, you should use these procedures under guidance of a professional, especially when you reach the point of calling attention to your heart.

5. Develop one skill before moving on to the next one. Begin with heaviness in the right arm before moving to the left. Then heaviness in both arms before moving to the right leg. Develop heaviness in both arms and both legs before moving to the feelings of warmth.

6. The formulae can be modified and words can be changed if they are easier for you to respond to. These modifications, however, are best made by someone who has the training to recognize what may be the underlying difficulty you are having with existing procedures.

7. It is possible to abbreviate the training period by omitting the last two formulae "My solar plexus is warm"; "My forehead is cool." These are not necessary for developing stress control.

8. Always end the procedures in the same way. Count

"one" to yourself and inhale; count "two" and stretch your arms and legs; count "three" and open your eyes.

As with meditation, begin by finding a quiet place where you can relax and won't be interrupted. The procedures should be practiced twice a day, and it is helpful if you have regularly scheduled times.

In contrast to meditation, autogenics can be practiced in either a sitting or reclining position. In both procedures it is usually best to have your eyes closed in order to reduce distractions. Some people even go so far as to cover their ears.

You will need about 15 minutes for each of your practice sessions (two per day). This is true even though you attend to the formulae for only 30-90 seconds. The reason is that within each session you practice 2-4 times, with two or three minutes between each period of concentration.

For example, in your very first session you would spend 30-90 seconds silently repeating, "My right arm is heavy." You would stop, take a deep breath on the count of one, stretch on the count of two, open your eyes, and resume a normal position on the count of three. After two or three minutes of quiet relaxation you would repeat the process.

Schultz and Luthe recommend that you keep a diary of your responses (physical, emotional, and intellectual) within each of the brief training periods. An entry might read something like: "September 22, 7 A.M. Practiced heaviness in my right arm. Unable to develop first time through. Second time began to experience a tingle in fingers; became excited and lost the feeling." The diary allows you to record progress. It serves as a reinforcer and is useful to an expert if some procedural modifications are indicated.

Many people take as long as a week of training, practicing every day, before they develop feelings of heaviness in their right arm. So if it takes a while, don't be discouraged. This is the most difficult time. You will be anxious at first, making it difficult to learn to be passive to distractions. This learning will transfer to the other formulae, and after developing heaviness in the right arm you will find things progressing more quickly. Often feelings of warmth begin to occur before you even get to that particular instruction.

As a brief rundown, the following should take place. Find a place, sit with your feet flat on the floor, arms on the side of a chair or in your lap. You may also lie down if it's more comfortable. Close your eyes and silently repeat, "My right arm is heavy," and continue to do this for about 90 seconds. Once you are able to accomplish a feeling of heaviness within 90 seconds you can add, "My left arm is heavy." Soon you will be able to say, "My right arm is heavy, my left arm is heavy, both arms are heavy." Once this is accomplished within 90 seconds, add, "My right leg is heavy," and then, "My left leg is heavy." In a short time you should be able to say, "My right arm is heavy, my left arm is heavy, both arms are heavy, my right leg is heavy, my left leg is heavy, both legs are heavy."

Once this goal has been reached the second formula should be added: "My right arm is heavy and warm." Stay with that suggestion until it develops, then proceed as above. Eventually you will reach the point of saying, "Both arms and both legs are heavy and warm." You will find that you are able to develop these feelings and the ones that follow all within the short time allowed.

Following heaviness and warmth you should introduce a suggestion of cardiac regularity: "Both arms and both legs are heavy and warm; my heart beat is calm and regular." As this occurs you should add a fourth suggestion dealing with respiration. "Both arms and both legs are heavy and warm; my heartbeat is calm and regular—it breathes me."

For many people "it breathes me" is an awkward phrase. The concept is that breathing is a spontaneous, natural process that happens on its own. You simply allow it, thus "it breathes me"—I don't breath it.

The fifth suggestion involves warmth in the solar plexus. "Both arms and both legs are heavy and warm, my heartbeat is calm and regular, it breathes me, my solar plexus is warm."

The final suggestion focuses on developing feelings of coolness in the forehead. "Both arms and both legs are heavy and warm, my heartbeat is calm and regular, it breathes me, my solar plexus is warm, and my forehead is cool."

This completes the autogenic phrases. Often this training provides the basis for engaging in some mental rehearsal of self-exploration (see Chapter 7). The exercises relax you, clear your mind enough to allow you to analyze and image more clearly and effectively. To do this, relax and before counting one, two, three to end the procedure, engage in the rehearsal process. Following rehearsal count one, two, three. Inhale on one, stretch on two, and resume normal activity on three.

More recently some individuals have been modifying Schultz's and Luthes' original procedures. Typically this has been to use the formula for warmth in the hands in order to treat migraine headaches. When this is the case, that single formula is often passively attended to for several minutes and will often be done while the person is simultaneously receiving biofeedback of finger temperature.

5

Biofeedback

Probably one of the most publicized procedures of the last decade is biofeedback. With its emphasis on objective measurement and its use of complicated electronics, this form of therapy fits nicely into our technical and mechanized world.

At its simplest level, biofeedback involves nothing more than a way to provide you with information about what is going on inside your body. Even taking your temperature and reading it is a form of biofeedback, as is sitting in a chair and taking your own pulse. These activities have gone on for a long time, yet no one became particularly excited about them.

The reason was that we didn't believe there was much we could do about the information once we received it. There was no notion that somehow we could gain enough control to alter what was happening inside of ourselves. Instead, we looked to our temperature or pulse rate as indications of how we were feeling at a particular time. If it were up, we would become worried and upset. If it were normal, we knew that all was okay for at least another day.

In the 1960s some research by Dr. Neale Miller at

Rockefeller University in New York began to change all of this. Working with laboratory rats, Dr. Miller was able to show that if you provided motivation for the animal to learn, it seemed to be able to get control over processes such as heart rate and blood flow, which were not believed to be under voluntary control.

Miller's early work aroused great interest, because it seemed possible that biofeedback might provide a way to teach humans to gain control over some of the physical processes that were associated with illness. The prospect, *as yet unfullfilled,* was that hypertense patients could be taught to lower their blood pressure, people with ulcers could be taught to decrease the amount of acid in their stomachs, and so on.

Later in the same decade biofeedback of human brain wave activity was investigated by Dr. Kamiya at Langley Porter Neuropsychiatric Institute. Kamiya had taken volunteers into his laboratory, connected them to equipment and measured what was going on in the brain. Kamiya had designed a feedback system so that the subject heard a tone only when he was producing alpha brain waves. His purpose was to see whether they could learn to control what was going on; so he asked them to try to maintain the tone.

It was back in the 1920s that a man named Berger had first recorded the activity of the brain. At that time he categorized brain wave activity on the basis of its frequence and amplitude. Alpha activity was between 8-13 cycles per second and had an amplitude of between 25 and 100 millionths of one volt. One of the observations Berger made was that alpha seemed to be present more often when subjects were relaxed, when they were not actively attending to some stimuli.

Somehow Kamiya's subjects seemed to be able to use the

feedback of the tone to learn to stay in the alpha state. They even began to report that they were experiencing a relaxed, passive attitude similar to that associated with meditation. Suddenly it looked as if biofeedback was the Western world's answer to Eastern meditation since it appeared that it was a direct way of measuring and teaching a meditative attitude.

The excitement generated by Kamiya and Miller's research gave birth to a new industry. Overnight companies were producing equipment designed to provide feedback of every bodily process imaginable. Biofeedback was applied to the treatment of everything from cancer to grinding of teeth.

At the present time a more sober view of the entire area has been taken. There does seem to be some real promise, but it is not the panacea initially imagined. Even the Food and Drug Administration has become involved in the area of biofeedback-regulating equipment. As it stands now, companies have to provide evidence to support all of the claims they make in their advertising. In addition, they are not supposed to sell equipment to consumers, but rather to professionals (M.D.s and psychologists).

You can go to a professional and have him prescribe equipment for you, or you can even build your own. The cost of most portable, reliable pieces of equipment, such as a unit to measure muscle tension, temperature or brain-wave activity, is between $300 and $1,000. You can build your own for approximately one third the cost.

But before you rush out to buy one, it may pay to find out what biofeedback can and can't do. It has been discovered that most of the control we thought people were getting over blood pressure and brain-wave activity from biofeedback can be attributed to that general relaxation response Benson talks about. Thus TM, autogenics, and a host of other procedures can allow you to relax and attain the same results. Blood pressure, respiration rate, heart rate, and skin-conductance level will all decrease while the amount of alpha activity in the brain will increase. So as a means of controlling hypertension, or for developing general relaxation, biofeedback is no more effective than the other methods.

It does appear that alpha, temperature in your fingers or muscle tension in your forehead, can all be used to teach you to relax. Since the feedback of finger temperature and of muscle tension also have some specific applications, it would make sense to buy equipment to provide this type of feedback first, before investing in brainwave feedback. Brain wave control sounds dramatic, and alpha has become an exciting word along with theta (another brain wave), but you would be better off saving your money.

A strong word of caution is needed here, since biofeedback is still being actively advocated. It is too easy to get carried away with the technology, to believe that science can accomplish anything. The equipment and atmosphere that surrounds biofeedback, in combination with a real signal telling you what is happening to your body, can be very supportive and helpful in establishing the confidence to reduce anxiety.

Getting rid of ingrained habits takes more than equipment, however, and it would be a gross misconception to think that all one needs to do is get hooked up to a machine and problems will solve themselves. Guidance is required, especially for more severe problems, and more often than not biofeedback is combined with some other form of treatment, such as progressive relaxation or autogenics.

In addition to teaching people to relax, biofeedback has specific application for the reduction of pain due to excessive muscle tension. It has also been used to treat vascular problems and migraine headaches. Research conducted on the biofeedback process, in fact, indicates that in a fairly short period of time, often only a few hours, individuals are able to learn to control various muscle groups and thus control their level of tension in particular areas. This has been a boon to those who have had to rely on drugs for pain reduction.

In our own laboratory treatments for muscle tension, migraine headaches, and fears (in which case biofeedback is combined with systematic desensitization) individuals usually require about 10 hours of training. Following this, if they continue to practice the relaxation exercise they have learned with the aid of biofeedback, they can retain whatever gains they have made in treatment without the use of the equipment.

It can be estimated that roughly 70 percent of the people treated for fears, muscle pain, and migraine headaches report significant improvement. The cost for a program ranges from $15 to $70 per session for a total of between $150 to $700.

The next two cases are presented to illustrate the specific application of biofeedback to pain. The first deals with a problem that orthopedists refer to as "overuse syndrome," which can occur because of excessive and improper use of muscles and tendons.

In the past, treatment had consisted of medication to reduce inflammation and instructions to abstain from the activity causing pain for an extended period of time. For a professional musician or athlete, whose life depends on performance, such instructions are almost impossible to follow, and the thought alone is enough to generate consideration stress. Biofeedback provides a means of combining medication with reducing muscle tension. The result is that practice often does not have to be discontinued.

The second case deals with the problem of back pain, an area that is a very common source of difficulty.

John had been exposed to music at a very early age, starting piano lessons even before his formal education. There was a great deal of emphasis on the importance of music and the ability to play at least one instrument within his family, which may have been the result of his mother's admiration for her sister, a professional opera singer. Additionally, John's uncle was a concert cellist. It was decided that John had a natural ability for music, and everything was done to encourage this aspect of his life. He was taken to concerts and operas regularly and continued his piano studies throughout his pre-teen years. There was no question in anyone's mind about what John would do when he grew up.

During high school and college John played in various ensembles and found that the organ provided greater musical tone and depth than the piano. This discovery led him to what he envisioned for himself upon graduation from his New England college: a musical career that was sure to be aided by his uncle's connections with numerous symphonic orchestras.

By the time John was 25 he had begun to play professionally, although he was striving for one last accomplishment—his master's degree. Thanks to his talent, he had never really felt much pressure while going through school, but this last attainment, the culmination of all his study and work, had caused him to become fairly anxious about the pieces he had chosen to play for his degree.

John decided to play a long Wagnerian passage as a part of his program. Although he was very familiar with the piece, he still felt considerable anxiety regarding his performance and had begun to over-practice in order to prepare himself.

As a result of his anxiety and the increased practice time,

John developed a severe inflammation in his elbow, which turned into a case of tendonitis. This not only interfered with his practice but also was the cause of a great amount of pain whenever he tried to play. It became so bad that John was afraid he wouldn't be able to play at all when the time came for his recital.

He felt that if he wasn't able to practice, he wouldn't be able to complete his program and accomplish what he so desperately wanted. This anxiety served only to aggravate the muscle tension and the tendonitis. His difficulty and accompanying concern were fortunately noticed by his instructor, who had dealt with similar problems in the past, and John was recommended to the biofeedback lab near the school.

John had seen demonstrations of its uses in one of his music classes, So, he was not only prepared in advance but also had some very positive expectancies regarding biofeedback's capabilities as a treatment. He knew its achievements in dealing with muscle tension, and he had a great deal of confidence in his instructor who had suggested the procedure.

John felt that his problem was only a physical one, not a psychologically caused dilemma. Biofeedback, with its sophisticated machinery, worked well within the framework of his conceptions. He began the six sessions that were designed to provide him with feedback of the muscle tension levels in his arm and specifically around his elbow. This was also combined with treatment for the actual inflammation.

The program designed for John offered him an opportunity to relax for 15 minutes, with an additional 10 minutes taken up with his visualizing himself playing the organ and making the small muscle movements required to finish the piece of music. In a short time John found that he was able to become very sensitive to the level of muscle tension he experienced and was able to relax them when they tensed.

This heightened sensitivity went a long way in reducing his pain, and John was able to continue his practicing at a moderate level. His concern regarding the tendonitis lessened, and he finished his recital and received the master's degree he had worked so hard to get.

Alex S. is a 55-year-old executive with a chemical company who has suffered from severe lower back pains due to excessive muscle tension. The fact that the nature of his work causes him to be fairly sendentary didn't help the problem, nor was the fact that he was slightly overweight and totally out of shape.

Taking a leave of absence from work when the pain became too intense, Alex entered into a biofeedback program. In conversation it was found that Alex had begun experiencing some conflicts over whether he could keep up with his work and concurrently was having a difficult time with his marriage. In terms of the latter problem, Alex and his wife were experiencing the same withdrawal pains since the last of their three daughters had gotten married and left the house. Suddenly alone together for the first time in 30 years, both were finding it difficult to sustain a relationship that had been so caught up with children for so long.

For Alex the problem went deeper partly because he had not maintained himself physically over the years. As most businessmen his age, he had neglected physical activity and instead concentrated on his work, using the weekends for sleep and watching sports programs on television. Doctors had told him that he had very tight muscles in the back of his legs and his lower back. He knew that he needed to be active to lose weight and get relaxed, but his tension, and the severity of it, had kept him from continuing any one exercise program for any length of time.

He had tried a number of different treatments for his

back alone, including heat therapy, back rubs, and massage; but nothing seemed to cure the pain. Out of desperation, to alleviate the pain in his legs, he had an operation to have the muscles surgically severed. This provided some immediate relief which then worsened after less than two days, forcing Alex to undergo the same painful experience another time with the same results.

For his lower back disorder Alex had been given injections of xylocaine, a derivative of novacaine, in conjunction with cortisone, an anti-inflammatory agent. This mixture was injected into his lower back, but it too was not successful in eliminating the pain.

It wasn't until Alex entered the biofeedback program that he began experiencing some longer-lasting results. The biofeedback was directed to his lower back, and he was able to relax the muscles in that area during his treatment, which lasted fifteen sessions, each approximately 45 minutes long. The lessening of muscle tension in his back provided him with an amount of relief he had not experienced before with any other technique.

Alex was also encouraged to begin practicing a progressive relaxation procedure at home to further solidify the positive results he was gaining from his biofeedback sessions. He was asked to focus on the feelings of tension in the muscles of his legs and lower back. Being a very disciplined man, Alex needed a sense of purpose for following particular procedures as well as reasonable explanations regarding why one method was better than another. No "far-out" type of procedure would have been acceptable to his particular values.

With biofeedback he had been well-prepared for the events that were to take place during the course of treatment, due to some public relations work his company had participated in as well as a television show he had seen, which showed individuals being helped for problems of muscle tension.

The introduction of progressive relaxation was handled in much the same way. Great care was taken to point out the work of Dr. Jacobson and his findings from experiments where he had applied electro-physiological apparatus to measure muscle tension. Supported by these facts, Alex was able to throw himself into the program with such faith and intensity that it was easy for him to exercise above and beyond the two days a week that were prescribed for him.

He made some dramatic improvements, not the least of which was a reduction in his weight, and began to enjoy a better relationship with his wife and a fuller life than before. The reduction in pain enabled him to pursue outside interests and hobbies that had long interested him.

In terms of practical usage beyond the previous examples, biofeedback can provide you with information about any of the processes going on in your body. It would be impossible for us to cover every application here, but we will tell you about two specific procedures. They are by far the most common and have the most research behind them. In addition, they have the most direct application to problems you might be interested in.

Feedback of muscle tension (EMG activity) is common, both as a treatment for specific muscular problems and as a method for teaching people to relax. In fact, the feedback of muscle-tension levels in your forehead (the frontalis muscles) is almost invariably used when training in relaxation is desired. This is the first type of feedback procedure we will explain in detail. The second procedure involves the feedback of finger temperature. This training is used in the treatment of migraine headaches.

Frontalis Muscle Tension

The following represents the step-by-step procedures you would go through if you walked into a laboratory in order to use biofeedback to learn to relax.

1. You would sit down in a comfortable chair and biofeedback would be explained to you. You would be told that the procedure being used involves attaching some electrodes to the frontalis muscles in your forehead. These are chosen above all other muscle groups because they provide a better indication of your general level or arousal. If you learn to relax these muscles the relaxation seems to generalize to your entire body. Reflection on this for a moment may provide you with an understanding of why this might be so. In our society we use our face to express our feelings. The equipment is very sensitive and can measure minute changes in facial-muscle tension that tend to reflect your level of arousal and anxiety.

2. The electrodes would be attached in the following fashion. Usually there are three disc electrodes. These are attached with adhesive (much like Band Aids). Two of the electrodes are referred to as active electrodes, meaning that the electrical activity that is going on between these two is what will be measured. The third electrode is a ground. The two active electrodes are attached about an inch above each eyebrow, directly in line with the pupil of the eye when you are looking straight ahead. The attachment is a simple and painless process.

3. The electrodes pick up the electrical activity in your frontalis muscles. This is usually on the order of one-

to ten-millionths of a volt. Different people will have different amounts of electrical activity, and you cannot assume that because your reading is five millionths and someone else's is three millionths that they are more relaxed. Some people will be very relaxed at one and very tense at five. Others will be relaxed at five and tense at ten. Through feedback you will find out your range of electrical activity, and what affects it. You'll learn what thoughts, feelings and events cause it to go up, and what causes it to go down.

4. The electrical activity is sent from the electrodes to the EMG, which amplifies it to the point that it is powerful enough to provide you with a feedback signal. Usually this comes to you in the form of a click.

5. Now that you're hooked up and hearing clicks, it is explained that electrical activity is accumulated until there is enough present to generate a click. The more tense you are the quicker the accumulation and the faster the click rate. Your task is to try and slow this rate down. You are told that you can try different strategies to do this and are asked to keep your eyes closed.

6. At this point you are given 15 minutes of feedback, any longer and you could become fatigued. As you listen for clicks the trainer may be providing you with ideas about things to try. He may say, "Some people find attending to their breathing helps slow down the clicks." He may tell you to attend to certain muscle groups, or if he sees you getting frustrated may tell you to stop trying so hard. If that is the case he will probably distract you from the task and show you that when you stop trying so hard the clicks will slow down by themselves. Throughout this he will be providing

encouragement, saying "good" when he notices that you are getting some control.

7. Usually 15 minutes of practice is followed by a discussion of your reactions, suggestions about where to go from here and other pointers. Often people are encouraged to practice a procedure like TM or progressive relaxation on a daily basis.

Finger Temperature Feedback

Training to increase finger temperature does not differ a great deal from the training just presented. Again, subjects receive 10 sessions of training, with actual feedback in each session lasting for 15 minutes and the remainder of the 50 minutes spent discussing the effects of training on symptoms.

It is not uncommon for subjects to learn within the first three or four sessions to relax enough to alter their finger temperature by 5 to 10 degrees. Once again, different people have different ranges of finger temperature. Some may go from 65 to 90 and others may go from 93 to 95. The feedback will help you discover your range and what affects it.

As a treatment for migraine headaches it has been found that if you can learn to sense the onset of a headache, and can then relax finger temperature, you can often keep the headache from developing.

When you enter a session you are asked to sit down in a reclining chair. A thermistor is then attached to the index finger of your non-preferred hand with a piece of tape so that the little ceramic disc at the tip is placed right over the center of the fingerprint. Relaxation causes more blood to flow to the peripheral blood vessels in the finger, and as blood flow to the finger changes so does temperature, The ceramic disc changes shape in response to change in temperature and the changes are transduced by the equipment into electrical signals. Those are fed back to you either in the form of clicks or as a visual signal on a meter which measures absolute temperature.

To be able to use temperature feedback you should have equipment and a meter that will reflect temperature changes of 1/20 of a degee or less. In the lab you'll sit quietly and do whatever you can to get the meter to register an increase in your temperature. The trainer serves the same kind of purpose as before.

As you can see from the descriptions, the procedures are really quite simple. The most difficult part is getting involved in the first place.

6

Progressive Relaxation

The fourth physical approach to stress reduction is a procedure called progressive relaxation. Closely aligned to autogenics in its design, progressive relaxation exercises were developed out of the research of Dr. Edmund Jacobson in Chicago, in the 1930s. Jacobson, like Schultz and Luthe, was interested in developing systematic procedures that people could use to relax.

Although both autogenics and progressive relaxation proceed in a systematic fashion, the similarity ends there. In progressive relaxation you are asked to focus attention on particular muscle groups. You begin usually with the arms, move to the legs, then to chest, neck, shoulders, and so on. As we will discuss later, there have been many modifications made to the basic procedure, and each of them seems to work. The preference for one version or another would depend on you and your goals.

In the more traditional procedures you practice the exercises once or twice a day for 20 minutes at a time. You begin by first tensing muscles in a particular area and then relaxing them. This tension-relaxation is important for some people, as initially it's very difficult for them to tell if muscles are tense or relaxed. Tensing-relaxing provides a contrast to teach them what they should feel as they relax.

In each training session you tense and relax each of the major muscle groups throughout the body. The particular order you choose does not appear to matter. Some people feel more comfortable moving from their toes to the top of their head, while others start with their arms, then legs, and move around. What is important is that you practice on a regular basis and use the same order each time.

Progressive relaxation has been useful in lowering general levels of arousal. In addition, the procedures have been popular with athletes. One reason is that the focus on muscle groups can be modified to emphasize those areas that are of particular importance.

Progressive relaxation procedures are also structured so that there is a regular program to follow. The feedback, both from the tensing and relaxing and from the fact that something occurs within the first session (in contrast to autogenics), serves to build confidence in the potential effectiveness of the procedures.

It is interesting to note that progressive relaxation does not come with the same warnings about chronic disease problems that autogenics do. This stems from two factors: First, the procedures have been used most often by healthy individuals. Second, they focus on muscle groups rather than on cardiac rate and/or breathing, and, we are far less concerned about a cramp or malfunction in some voluntary muscle group than we are about something going wrong with our heart or lungs.

Should you decide that you want some supervision most clinical psychologists are familiar with the procedures. It is also possible to buy commercially prepared relaxation tapes. In a later section we have listed some places for you to write to if you are interested. Prices for the tapes range from around $9.95 to $40.00.

We have already mentioned that progressive-relaxation

procedures have had application to athletic situations. In addition, these procedures have also been used by individuals to combat problems of insomnia. They are practiced in a reclining position, so it is fairly easy to fall asleep. In addition, the focusing on different muscle groups (it is a "passive focusing," by the way) serves like a mantra to distract you from those thoughts and feelings that might be keeping you from sleeping. This is illustrated nicely in the case of Paul.

At 22, Paul was a small-town boy who had made the big time. He was a professional athlete who, prior to the time he left high school, had never been away from home. For the most part he had lived a very sheltered and secure life in a small Midwestern town.

He found it difficult to adapt to the life of a professional baseball player. It had its exciting times, but somehow Paul was unable to enjoy all of the travel. He would not admit outright fear (that would not have fit the image he had of himself), but he did indicate that he was unable to relax on flights, and the team made a great many. In addition, he found it very difficult to sleep in strange cities.

If Paul had been like many other people he might have admitted the fear of being alone. He might have confessed that all of the violence he read about, all of the weird-looking people he saw, made him uncomfortable. If that were the case, and if he stayed in one city long enough to go through a series of about 10 treatment sessions, he would have been able to be desensitized to his anxiety.

As it was, Paul would not admit his fear, only to being unable to rest, to being bothered by noises and the other players. Paul would not have come in for treatment if his coach hadn't insisted. He had noticed that particularly on long road trips his left fielder's playing tended to suffer.

Paul's treatment consisted of one 45-minute session.

During that time he was taken through the progressive relaxation procedures. He was given a cassette tape of the procedures that he had just gone through, with the only difference between the 15-minute tape and what Paul went through in the office being that the tensing part of the exercises were dropped.

Paul had indicated that he was aware of increases in his muscle tension. Thus the tensing was unnecessary, and in fact would only serve to keep him awake. The procedures were put on tape for Paul to listen to, rather than asking him to learn them and say them silently to himself, for a specific reason. It was felt that the voice on tape would give him something outside of himself to focus on and would cover up the noise on the plane and in the hotel rooms.

Paul did use the tape and found it very helpful, especially on the airplane. He even started using the procedures on his own, reporting that he had forgotten the recorder for one trip and had found that he didn't need it. From that time on he was fine.

The second case using progressive-relaxation procedures involved a college shot putter. When we first saw Ron he was already the conference champion. He had set a record early in his junior year of 52'3", and throughout the remainder of the track season was unable to improve on that mark.

Ron was a very dedicated and disciplined athlete. He wanted to be a coach and was a student of both the mental and physical aspects of the game. After the season ended he established an impressive physical training program for himself which he maintained through the summer and fall. By the winter of his senior year he had increased his strength considerably. In spite of being able to lift more weight, however, Ron found that through the first half of the season he was still unable to improve on his record.

As shot putters go Ron was not big. He was 6'2" and weighed 210 pounds. He had worked extensively on his technique and form, and his coaches indicated that they thought he was putting the shot about as far as he was physically capable of. Ron's peformance was very consistent—he almost invariably would have at least one put around 52 feet in each meet.

When he came in for treatment his dedication and thirst for knowledge were well suited to progressive-relaxation procedures. He was informed that even small amounts of anxiety and arousal could result in a general tension in his neck and shoulder muscles. Some of the tension would be in muscles that were antagonistic to putting the shot. He was told that if he could get these particular muscles relaxed he would get greater distance.

It is important to make several points here. First, Ron's level of arousal in competition was not that high, but it did not have to be to interfere. It was not high enough to be perceived as fear, so a procedure such as desensitization was unnecessary. In addition, Ron did not need to improve his technique, thus mental rehearsal or some of the cognitive procedures were not necessary. Ron's attitude was fine—all he needed to do was reduce muscle tension in his neck and shoulders. Progressive relaxation was the perfect procedure, and Ron found that he had plenty of time to go through the exercises just prior to competing.

As with Paul there was only one session. Ron was taught the procedures and given a written set of instructions. He was told to practice the procedures regularly twice a day and just before competition.

Two weeks after starting the relaxation procedures Ron set a new conference record, putting the shot 52 feet 7 inches. In the final meet of the season, a week later he reached 53 feet.

As we tried to show by these two case histories, progressive relaxation, like the other relaxation procedures, requires you to be able to adopt a passive attitude toward any distractions that occur during the practice. This passive response to irrelevant thoughts, combined with conscious attempts to relax successive groups of muscles, is all that you need do. Progressive relaxation should be practiced every day for about 15 minutes at a time, and by learning to relax under non-stressful conditions you should eventually find yourself gaining more control when under pressure.

When progressive relaxation procedures were first introduced they stressed an individual's ability to tense a particular muscle and then relax it. We will not do that here. It has been our experience that most subjects do not need the tensing part of the exercise. The goal with progressive relaxation, like autogenic training, is for you to be able to commit the procedures to memory and then to be able to apply them whenever and wherever you want to. If you find it difficult at first you might read the following exercise onto a tape. Keep in mind, however, that you want to learn to relax without listening to the tape.

Step I

Find a comfortable place where you will not be disturbed. You may either sit or lie down, loosen any restricting clothing and remove glasses or contact lenses.

Step II

Close your eyes and begin by inhaling deeply and exhaling slowly . . . inhale deeply and exhale slowly. Now as you exhale, relax all of the muscles in your right arm. Relax the muscles in your fingers, wrist, forearm, and upper arm. Completely relax all of the muscles in your right arm. Notice that as you relax the muscles in your right hand and arm and as you exhale, how much heavier the arm becomes. Pay attention to the increased heaviness in your arm as you relax and exhale. Fine, now relax the muscles in your left arm. Relax your fingers . . . your wrist . . . your forearm and your upper arm. Completely relax all of the muscles in your left arm. As before, notice when you exhale the increased heaviness as your arm relaxes and presses down against your chair. Continue to breathe deeply and slowly, inhaling deeply . . . and exhaling slowly, and as you do, notice the feelings of heaviness in the muscles in both arms.

Now relax the muscles in your right leg. Relax the muscles in the foot and toes . . . in the ankle . . . in the calf . . . and in the thigh. Now relax all of the muscles in your right leg, in your right arm . . . and in your left arm. Just completely relax and let yourself go. Now relax the muscles in your left leg. Relax the muscles in your foot and toes. Relax the muscles in your ankle . . . your calf . . . and in your thigh. Relax the muscles in both arms and both legs, and notice as you exhale the increased heaviness in your arms . . . and legs . . . as you let yourself go . . .

That's fine. If your mind wanders while relaxing that's all right, just notice it and come back to the exercise. Don't become upset. Just relax and come back to attending to the feelings as you relax. Now relax the muscles in your face. Relax your forehead. Relax the muscles around your eyes . . . and in your jaw. Let your mouth open slightly as you completely relax the muscles in your face . . . and jaw. That's fine. Continue breathing deeply and slowly. Notice the increased heaviness in your body as you completely relax the muscles in your arms ... legs ... face ... and jaw. Now relax the muscles in your neck and in your shoulders.

Relax the muscles in your chest. Notice the pleasant sensations as you completely relax and let yourself go. Relax all of the muscles in your arms ... your legs. Relax the muscles in your shoulders ... and chest. Now relax the muscles in your stomach ... and abdomen. Just completely relax and let yourself go.

Breathe deeply and slowly and enjoy the feelings of deep relaxation as you relax all of the muscles in your right arm, in the fingers ... wrist ... forearm ... and upper arm. Relax all of the muscles in your left arm ... in your fingers ... wrist ... forearm ... and upper arm. Relax the muscles in both legs ... in the feet ... ankles ... calves and thighs. Relax the muscles in your face ... and forehead ... and jaw. Relax the muscles in your neck ... and shoulders. Relax the muscles in your chest ... and abdomen. Relax the muscles in your entire body.

Insert rehearsal here

That's fine. Continue to relax for the next few minutes. When you are ready to get up, count "one" and take a deep breath. Count "two" and stretch your arms and legs. Count "three" and open your eyes and move your body. When you are ready to get up, count "one" to yourself and take a deep breath. Count "two" silently and stretch your arms and legs. Count "three" . . . open your eyes, and resume your normal activity.

This concludes the progressive relaxation procedure. The whole practice should take from between 15 to 20 minutes. You will also remember that we indicated relaxation was often combined with cognitive rehearsal procedures. The relaxation makes the imagery more intense and vivid and helps improve concentration. Should you be incorporating both relaxation and imagery into your program, the latter would be inserted where we have indicated. Even with the imagery included you should limit the rehearsal to not more than 25 minutes, including relaxation time. Usually, the same 15-20 minute period is enough, particularly as you become more skillled at inducing feelings of relaxation.

This concludes the section on physical relaxation procedures. We will discuss other applications of some of these same procedures in later chapters when we present some cases that combine two or more treatment approaches.

In the next section of the book we will provide you with information about several different ways you can gain more control over your own attitude and mental processes. As mentioned earlier, the physical procedures tend to focus on physical change, with the assumption that attitude will change as well. For example, once Ron put the shot farther he felt better. The procedures that are presented next assume that if you can alter your thinking and attitude, your body will follow along.

Part Three:

HOW TO IMPROVE PHYSICAL PERFORMANCE

In Chapters 3 through 6 we dealt with procedures that were primarily concerned with the prevention and treatment of physiological responses to stress. However, the effects of stress aren't always physical. Some of us react to pressure differently, becoming confused, overloaded or, even panicky. We begin to get down on ourselves, lose confidence and become less effective. Many of us are so dominated by a loss of self-esteem and feelings of worthlessness that those symptoms become far more important than any physical reactions.

If we have a backache or headache, we're conditioned to take a pill. Even when we find ourselves in a frightening situation and our heart starts to beat rapidly, or we start to perspire, we understand that "It's only natural." We are able to accept the physical response and as a result it doesn't get out of control.

Mental reactions to stress, however, attack us in a different way. The loss of confidence, feelings of worthlessness and inadequacy are not so easy to deal with. Often these feelings seem to be there for no reason. We walk into a final exam and know that all of the answers are right in our head. We also know that the teacher wants us to do well, but somehow, in spite of all of this, we find ourselves panicking. We look at the test and our mind becomes blank. We feel confused as we jump from one thought to another. With our concentration impaired, all the knowledge we *know* we have is no longer at our command. We become frustrated, angry, begin to think that there is something wrong with us and lose confidence in our own abilities.

The procedures in the previous chapters were designed to help you handle inappropriate physical responses to pressure. The methods you will be exposed to now are therapies for those of us who suffer self-defeating mental responses to stress.

7

Mental Rehearsal and Cybernetics

In this chapter we will talk about both mental rehearsal and the procedures Maxwell Maltz has called *Psycho Cybernetics*. In essence they both recognize that skill, as well as attitude, is important in determining success. Both of them are based on the assumption that mental practice can improve physical performance. For additional information on these particular procedures you might refer to Dr. Maltz's book and to a book by the co-author on the psychology of athletics entitled *The Inner Athlete* (Robert M. Nideffer, published by T.Y. Crowell).

Most of us engage in some kind of mental rehearsal from time to time. This may range from the subvocal rehearsing of a speech we must deliver to extensive visualization of some upcoming situation. Often we impose on the visualization process our own outcomes, and ideally we view ourselves as being successful, though this isn't always the case.

There has been a variety of research that supports the usefulness of mental rehearsal. Simple correlational studies have shown that the more successful athletes not only have better recall of their performance, but that they are able to visualize more accurately the layout of a course or the actual competitive situation than less successful individuals.

Coaches who have used systematic rehearsal procedures with athletes have reported that they can learn new and complicated activities approximately two to four times as fast as they can if they engage in physical practice alone. It really is possible to improve your skill by thinking about it. The important thing is being able to develop the rehearsal ability and knowing what to rehearse.

Depending upon what is rehearsed, the procedure can focus more on attitude change or skill building. With positive thinking the emphasis is on changing attitudes. With this type of rehearsal you concentrate on how you want to feel, or on what you want to have happen. Many times the self instructions are verbal, "You will win." When visualization occurs, it involves seeing yourself as a winner.

A procedure that follows skill building would be the type that a basketball player like Pete Maravich engages in. He goes home *after* a game and replays every minute. He concentrates on mentally correcting his mistakes and emphasizing what he did right. Some of our Olympic coaches use the same techniques to teach gymnastics and diving skills. This same type of rehearsal is even being incorporated into programs designed to develop interviewing skills, public-speaking techniques, impulse control, and better parenting ability.

An example of a rehearsal process that encompasses both skill building and development of a positive attitude would be that of Dwight Stones, the world-class high jumper. His deliberate style before his jumps bears out the proposition of mental rehearsal. You can actually see Stones moving his head and eyes as he counts out the steps that he will take in approaching the bar.

Stones provides a good example of the rehearsal process

because you can understand, through his facial movements, what it is that he sees. Often the process is not so discernable. Another individual who uses rehearsal is Vasilia Alexiev, the world record holder in weight lifting. Just prior to a lift it is easy to see that Alexiev is pulling himself together, but what he is visualizing as he does so is not observable.

Athletic examples provide dramatic evidence of the rehearsal process, but one doesn't need to be involved in competitive athletics to utilize mental rehearsal. Each of us has many areas where a systematic rehearsal would improve our performance: The young man may be less shy if he visualizes how he is going to behave on a date. The businessman getting ready to give an important speech may, in the course of practicing his talk, benefit from visualizing the setting and the expression on people's faces as he is talking. The housewife preparing a special dinner for her family may do a better job if she *knows* what the final meal will look like and how the table will be set.

If the rehearsal process sounds easy, it's because it is. There are, however, some complications. First, just as one can rehearse successes and achieve them, one can also rehearse and develop failures. Some of us have a great deal of difficulty in visualizing ourselves as successful.

Two cases illustrate the above point quite nicely. In the first instance a young girl came in because she had fallen apart in several job interviews. She would fail to hear questions correctly, often responding only to the first part of any query. She would become confused and would start talking very rapidly and, at times, not even relate what she was saying to the question.

When she was asked to rehearse herself in a job interview—waiting for questions, responding slowly and so on, she was unable to do so. Even the thought of the situation was so anxiety-inducing that she could not visualize it, at least not successfully.

In her instance two things had to be done. First, she had to learn to relax, and so we used one of the procedures presented in Part One. Next, she had to learn to perform in a successful way. Thus, role-playing situations were created where she actually went through mock interviews, beginning first with very non-threatening ones. Once she found she was capable of positive behavior, and once her attention was called to her feelings at that time, she was able to then visualize successfully and rehearse.

The second situation involved a professional field goal kicker who wanted to use rehearsal to improve the consistency of his kicking. When he was first asked to visualize himself kicking, he saw himself trying to kick a 50-yard field goal in the last minutes of a crucial game, and on a wet field. He slipped as he approached the ball and missed. But because he had success in the past with more routine kicks, it was easier to deal with his problem. He was asked first to rehearse extra-point kicks, then short, non-crucial field goals. Soon he was able to visualize more difficult kicks, which raised his average on the field.

The ability to rehearse mentally is something that we can all develop in order to speed the learning process and help increase self-confidence. What is critical is to create the conditions to facilitate the rehearsal process. Often this involves finding a time when we are relaxed and comfortable, or else we must teach ourselves to relax. The relaxation acts to reduce distractions and to improve our imagery.

A second critical factor is to know what it is that we should rehearse. As we suggested earlier, the simple rehearsal of positive self-statements often is not enough. You have to realistically look at your goals as well as your abilities. Chances are if what you want to do is simply improve the consistency of your performance, you already have the skills and know what to do. Under these circumstances you can design your own rehearsal program.

On the other hand, if your goal is to improve performance in order to achieve a level that you have not yet experienced, then you may need help to identify what it is you should be doing. In that case, what you'll need is a good teacher, coach or book to help you identify that.

A caution should be introduced here. Mental rehearsal can be overdone as well as underdone. The individual who makes the same mistakes over and over again may not be reflective and analytical enough to recognize mistakes. Rehearsal could help. On the other hand, it is possible to become so captivated by seeing yourself doing things, and by providing yourself with positive instructions, that you are engaging in this when you should be paying attention to the actual game or business situation.

Sometimes anxiety makes us over-rehearse. In tennis, for example, we may be so busy anticipating and visualizing how we are going to return the serve that we don't see the ball coming until it's too late.

The over-rehearsal of the salesman causes him to go ahead with the same old sales pitch even though the customer is giving ample evidence of disinterest in what he has to say. He loses the sale only because he fails to see the warning signs.

It is equally important to pick the right times to rehearse. Billy Jean King can be talking to herself just before her opponent tosses up the ball for the serve and stop within a fraction of a second. She has the luxury of rehearsing during a game. Others are less fortunate. They start to rehearse some situation and find themselves trapped, still thinking about it when the game goes on. If this is your problem, learn one of the passive-attention procedures in Part I and identify at what point in key situations that you can profitably rehearse.

Mental rehearsal involves little more than a step-by-step review of whatever it is that you want to practice or learn. What you actually "see" as you rehearse depends on you and on how much you practice. We will describe several ways people rehearse and then make suggestions that you can learn to practice.

1. Some people function in a very detached way, watching their own performance and reacting to it externally. This is similar to watching someone else perform.

2. Some individuals are more actively involved in what is going on. They are internally driven and see their performances more closely and emotionally. In rehearsing, they are the athlete, they are not watching a movie. In either instance, the goal is to attend actively to the critical aspects of performance and to attend passively to any interruptions. This is much like progressive relaxation, except that what you have to attend to is much more complex.

3. Some individuals are capable of moving from an external to an internal focus and back again almost at will, depending on the circumstance. This allows several advantages. You get yourself used to the perspective you will actually be in, but you also see yourself as others see you.

4. What is rehearsed varies from person to person and should depend on what it is you are trying to accomplish. It is possible to rehearse an activity just visually. You can also learn (as a participant) to call your attention to minute changes in muscle tension

levels associated with actual feelings and sensations of any performance activity.

5. Movement of the rehearsal process will depend on what you are trying to do. If you are an observer all of the time it can proceed much like a movie, with you controlling the speed and direction of the camera and action. If you are a participant then you may find the action proceeding in discrete sections. You'll notice, experience and feel one part of the activity, then break and attend to another part. Both types of rehearsal are most helpful for learning and that is what we will ask you to do in the examples that follow.

The most important aspect of the rehearsal process involves learning what it is that you should rehearse. We mentioned that if all you want to do is improve the consistency of your performance you probably know what it is that you need to attend to. In this instance you carefully outline the critical elements involved and systematically rehearse them. On the other hand, if you wish to improve your skill beyond your current level, you must learn new behaviors. Often you don't know what those behaviors are and need a teacher or coach to point them out to us. This is a critical point and is dealt with in detail in *The Inner Athlete*.

We are going to present two general examples of the rehearsal process. One of them deals with helping you rehearse your tennis forehand stroke. (Non-tennis players should have no trouble in transferring these directions to any other physical activity.) We will not attempt to coach you, but instead ask you to examine what it is that you actually do. If you find that you cannot develop the images asked for, stand up, go through the actual stroke a couple of times, then sit down and try again. Usually with this type of practice your memory should be helped to the point where you can eliminate the problem.

The second rehearsal process involves getting you to practice your behavior within a job interview situation. Here we point out what we believe are some important factors. In both instances, to facilitate the process you might first relax and then rehearse. In fact, you can read the rehearsal procedures (or your own instructions for other situations) onto the relaxation tape. Just place them where it says, "Insert rehearsal here."

Tennis Forehand

Step I
Find a comfortable, quiet spot. Sit down and relax.

Step II
Imagine that you are standing back near the base line. Your opponent is now swinging at the ball and you can see that it is going to be within easy reach on your forehand side. You will have to move only two or three steps to get into position.

Keeping your eye on the ball, begin moving to set up for the shot. Watch as it hits about two feet in back of the service line. By this time you are in position and have brought your racquet back. Stop all the action at this point and take a look at yourself. How are you holding the racquet? What grip are you using? Where is the racquet relative to your body and the ball? What is the position of your left leg and foot? Is the knee bent? What about your right leg and hips? What position is your body relative to the net? How is your weight distributed between your two legs at this point? Are your eyes on the ball? Fine. Now bring the racquet forward, to make contact with the ball and stop again.

Again check your position. Now, how is your weight distributed? What position is the racquet in relation to your body and the ball? How are you holding the racquet? What position is your head in? Where are your shoulders and hips pointing?

OK, swing through and watch as the ball makes contact with the face of the racquet. As you follow through what happens to your body? Notice and feel the shift in your weight as you move into and through the ball. What position are your feet in? Are you starting to bring your back foot forward? What is the position of your head, your hips, your shoulders? Fine. Now get ready to set up for the next shot as your opponent returns your shot.

You can make your own modifications to the rehearsal process by emphasizing various points, depending on your own desire and needs. You might work on a serve, lob, backhand, or focus on the placement of your shot so that you watch your movements as you attempt to place a shot down the line.

Job Interview

The procedures that we are going through here are presented not as the way to approach all job interviews, but as an example of how interpersonal contacts can be rehearsed. Different situations will require different behaviors.

Step I

Find a comfortable spot. Sit down, close your eyes and relax.

Step II

We want you to rehearse seeing yourself engage in certain behaviors in interview situations. We want you to practice these behaviors so that when you walk into an actual interview they will be automatic. Some of the things we will ask you to do may be natural for you anyway. If that is the case, great. We will ask you to attend to some details that may seem obvious or silly; however, they have been found to be important.

Imagine that you are walking into a reception area. You walk up to the receptionist and introduce yourself by saying, "Hello, my name is _____. I have an appointment with _____." The receptionist says, "I'll tell them you're here. Please have a seat."

You sit down, and as you do you are aware of several important factors. First, you showed up a few minutes early. You are clean, well groomed and dressed appropriately for the type of interview you are about to go through. If you are applying for a teaching or professional position, you look the part. You have done some checking in advance to determine the image the company or group expects.

The door opens and the interviewers ask you to come in. You stand up and walk toward them. They introduce themselves. You smile, tell them your name and shake hands (if they have extended theirs). When you shake hands you make sure you grip their hands firmly and look them in the eye.

You stand politely and wait for them to indicate where you should sit. If they give you a choice, select a seat that allows you to be more directly involved in the interview. Don't place a lot of distance or furniture between you and the other persons.

They begin by asking you a general question, and you handle the answer the way you will with all the others to follow: Unless its meaning is obvious you restate it, altering the words slightly, in order to be sure that you heard the question correctly. In addition, if it is very general and you are not sure what they are looking for, you ask for a little more structure.

For example, the first question might be, "Tell me about yourself." A good answer would be, "I would love to; where would you like me to begin?" You'll find out whether they want a complete biography or just your work history. Before going to the interview you have tried to do a little homework to find out about the job, the responsibilities, and the company or area in general. You have also tried to think about the abilities and experiences that you have had which would make you an asset to the company. The general question allows you to display both of these.

Most companies expect to provide beginning workers with the training they need to handle a job. Therefore, your objective in the interview is to convince the person of your ability to learn, your motivation, and your good character.

"How is it that you are interested in this job?"

"I am glad you asked that question. For as long as I can remember I have wanted to be a teacher. Although this would be my first teaching job, I have worked as a student teacher before and feel that I bring my own excitement and enthusiasm to the class. I think I have an ability to communicate."

As you are talking, pay particular attention to how you are sitting. You should be comfortable and relaxed, but you should not be slouching back in your chair. You should be sitting upright, leaning slightly toward the interviewer. You should be making frequent eye contact and smiling when it seems appropriate. Your hands are in your lap and used occasionally for gestures or to make a point. Make sure that they do not get in front of your face.

Watch the interviewers for cues. If they look like they are getting restless while you're talking, stop. Ask them, "Is that what you had in mind?" If they say "yes" then ask if they have heard enough or if they would like you to continue. It is easy to pick up cues from the interviewers when you are watching them as you talk, so don't talk to the floor.

As the interviewers signal that it is time to end the session, stand up and wait for them to direct you out. If a hand is offered, shake it warmly, look them in the eye and thank them for their time.

The presentation you just went through is very general. The more you know about a given job or interviewer, the more specific you can be in what you rehearse. The important thing to remember is to behave in a way that communicates interest, enthusiasm, and a willingness and ability to learn. This is most easily accomplished when you watch the interviewer. Let them provide structure. You can help by rephrasing their questions and then sharpening your responses by asking if that was what they had in mind.

8

Self-Hypnosis

Procedures such as cybernetics and mental rehearsal are relatively simple and can be successfully employed by a great many of us. These procedures, however, contain no real promise of providing something extra, outside of ourselves. We must have faith in our own ability, which at times can be very difficult to develop and maintain. If this is true in your case, then self-hypnosis might be a helpful alternative to mental rehearsal, or even to positive thinking.

Self-hypnosis, like hypnosis (which we will discuss later) is a mysterious, almost magical procedure to many people. The stories we have heard, perhaps the demonstrations we have seen, all support the notion that with hypnosis we can transcend our own abilities. It is as if the trance state gives us abilities that wouldn't be there if we relied on more conventional techniques. For some of us the faith we can place in hypnosis and not in ourselves is the critical ingredient to successful change. This belief alone can sometimes allow us to function closer to our ultimate potential. In actuality, we don't transcend our abilities, we only think we do.

Self-hypnosis can be ideal for those of us who want to

bridge the gap between doing something ourselves rather than having someone else do it for us. In practice, you can learn self-hypnosis from books like this one, from the purchase of records and tapes, or by going to a hypnotist and having him teach you. If confidence is a key factor then it would be worthwhile going to the hypnotist, though you should find out specific details before you sign up for the course.

Self-hypnosis, by its very design, can give additional support against pain or emotional pressures that may arise. Since it involves a certain amount of time and dedication in order to be effective, self-hypnosis is not a methodology for everyone and for every type of problem. What does make it attractive for a variety of people is the mystical aura associated with it.

Self-hypnotic procedures have had a great deal of successful application in reducing pain during childbirth, and in helping individuals break habits such as smoking and excessive eating. Hypnotists are free to advertise in the yellow pages, although psychologists and psychiatrists who use hypnosis are unable to do so because of their professional ethics. Both the International Society of Clinical and Experimental Hypnosis and the Society of Clinical and Experimental Hypnosis will provide names of members who use hypnosis in treatment. These addresses are presented in Chapter 13.

If you think self-hypnosis is a procedure for you and decide you want to receive some expert training, here are some points you should consider.

1. Anybody can call himself a hypnotist. Unlike the professional labels of psychologist or psychiatrist; the title "hypnotist" is not protected by law.
2. Make it a point to find out the individual's background

and training. Membership in an association or certification by some society may look impressive, but it may have been purchased for $20 or have been given because of participation in a two-day workshop. You can learn hypnotic techniques in a few hours; however, long professional training is needed to develop the ability to evaluate whether self-hypnosis is appropriate for a given individual. The more you feel a need for outside support the more important it will be to see someone with that extensive training.

3. Find out what is being taught; how many sessions are required, and what the charge is for each session. Typical fees range from $15 to $40 per session. A program that includes helping you lose weight or stop smoking can be expected to require more sessions than one that simply teaches the technique of self-hypnosis. The latter can be learned in one or two sessions, although many hypnotists will insist you take time to learn about hypnosis (which is a good idea), about its potential benefits and dangers as well as its technique. It's a little like requiring so many hours of ground school for pilots. Flying skill isn't developed there, but the understanding necessary to avoid and cope with dangerous situations is.

4. If you are interested in self-hypnosis for the treatment of an addictive problem such as smoking or overeating, many hypnotists already have well-developed programs for these common problems. They should be able not only to teach you to induce a hypnotic state, but also what to do and say to yourself once there.

Unfortunately, if you want to use it for help in a less common area, the hypnotist may be far less helpful. The real tragedy is that often hypnotists don't recognize their own limitations. One who expects to help an athlete improve performance or a businessman improve his speaking or negotiation skills must know what is required. In many cases you, the patient, are going to be more of an expert in the area of your problem than he is. So find out what the professional has to offer you in terms of a) technique; b) background for understanding your problem, both from a psychological and from a physical or technical point of view.

Under the right circumstances self-hypnosis can be very useful, as the following cases illustrate.

Roger has always had difficulty in controlling his weight. By the sixth grade he was the fattest kid in class. Throughout high school the problem had persisted although he was forever trying to find the one diet that would help. Because of his weight he gave up trying to be active socially or athletically. Now 30, he had begun to feel that there was no hope and that the problem was hereditary although no one else in his family was overweight. His family had long since stopped pressuring him to lose weight when they realized that all their pressure did was make Roger more anxious, thus causing him to eat more.

Diets seemed only to sensitize him to food. Each time he would start a diet he would be psyched up to get the results he wanted. Then the first thought that would pop into his mind was that he wasn't supposed to eat. This in turn would make him hungry, and before he knew it he was raiding the refrigerator.

After high school Roger went into the service, and soon his weight dropped down to a normal level. He felt good about himself, and his self-confidence increased. Unfortunately, the control was tied to the structure of the military. Access to food was limited, both in terms of proximity and time. In addition, exercise was imposed. However, as soon as he returned to civilian life his weight once again began to balloon.

Through the years Roger's weight went up and down like a yo-yo. Whenever it was down, it was because the environment was structured in such a way as to control his food intake. In college he was actively involved in classes and also participated in athletics for the first time. These involvements kept his weight under control for a couple of years. At the end of his senior year, however, he gained 30 pounds in three months and then added another 30 over the next year. Suddenly he had gone from 160 to 220 pounds.

Roger wanted to lose weight, but his physical activity had dropped once again because he was too embarrassed to be seen by others. The one positive thing was that he had become involved in coaching ·children in Little League baseball and had begun playing with them.

At the same time his wife began exerting more pressure by not bringing fattening snacks home and by controlling the menu. Again his weight fell because of these external supports, but as soon as the season was over Roger began cheating on his diet. His wife, out of frustration, eventually gave up on trying to control things at home. Why should she eat nothing but spinach because her husband was fat?

By the time he had reached 220 pounds for the fourth time in his life, Roger was ready for anything that could help. He turned to self-hypnosis. Fortunately, Roger was a good hypnotic subject (not everyone is). The program that he became involved in consisted of 25 sessions. In the first few sessions Roger learned about hypnosis and also developed his understanding, confidence, and faith in both himself and the procedures. The next few sessions involved teaching Roger a hypnotic-induction technique that he could use on himself. With some very good subjects a post-hypnotic suggestion given by the hypnotist is often all that is needed.

For example, you might be hypnotized by someone and be instructed that after you wake up you will find that you can induce hypnosis in yourself by just sitting down in a particular chair and counting to three. The second way to learn is to take yourself through an entire hypnotic-induction procedure. In a sense, you are saying the same things to yourself the hypnotist might say.

The third part of Roger's training consisted of giving him specific instructions that were designed to alter his self-motivation and actual eating behavior. He was told, for example, to visualize himself the way he *wanted* to look. He was to see himself as being thin and attractive and was given instructions for countering his hunger pangs. "You will not feel hungry but will find yourself feeling satisfied after eating only a few bites." Finally, he was given suggestions for countering the negative "I can't" or "I'll start tomorrow" thoughts.

A brief comment is appropriate here. Often, self-hypnotic suggestions are of a more general nature, much like the power of positive thinking statements, with the addition of the mystical aspect that is so much a part of hypnosis. As the suggestions become more specific and begin to focus on particular thoughts, self-hypnosis begins to take on many of the characteristics of cognitive behavior modification, which will be dealt with in the next chapter.

Roger was able to use the program successfully to maintain a weight loss. He has kept his weight down (in spite of the fact that his job required him to eat out often with clients) for the past five years. He continues to use self-hypnosis and in addition attends a group meeting (with other graduates of the program) once a month.

The second case involves the use of hypnogogic images

and a variation of self-hypnosis. Hypnogogic images develop quite naturally when you simply allow yourself to relax, close your eyes and attend to what is going on behind your eyelids. For most of us there is a small amount of pressure on the eyeball when we close our eyes. As a result we may see little spots of light or cloud-like formations called phosphene images. If you lie quietly and passively attend to these images they will begin to move, change shape, and you may often be spontaneously presented with a perception (in surprising clarity) of an object or situation. You may be lying there, for example, and suddenly see a pair of binoculars, chicken, house, farm scene, or any number of things. With some patience and guidance this situation can be used much like traditional self-hypnosis.

With practice it is possible to gain control over these images in order to shape them to your liking and thus make them do what you want them to (much like seeing yourself as thin). You should be warned, however, that occasionally the images that develop can be startling. One woman saw herself stabbing someone. If you get past those minor distractions you can learn to develop your own programs.

Jerry was a 34-year-old postal employee who had to pass tests for promotions. He had come in for help because he had twice failed an exam which was a necessary step in his career plans. The test consisted of having to sit in front of a machine that rapidly presented letters. Jerry was required to scan the letters quickly, and depending on their markings, push buttons that sorted the material for different areas.

The first two times Jerry had tried to pass the test his anxiety got so out of hand that he felt as if the letters were coming at him faster than it was humanly possible to handle. He became overloaded, confused, and totally unable to deal with the testing situation.

Talks with Jerry, and the fact that he had already been through two failures, would seem to indicate that his level of self-confidence was so low that simple relaxation procedures would not do the job. Hypnogogic images were used. The procedure of sitting quietly while passively attending to information was explained to Jerry. As images began to develop, and he gained greater control, he was encouraged to shape them so that they described the testing situation.

In about sixteen sessions Jerry learned to visualize the machine and to control the rate of presentation of the material. He was encouraged to practice on his own each day and was left with the expectancy that such practice would result in his successfully passing the test.

When Jerry took the test for the third time he had no trouble at all. In fact, he reported that it seemed as if the machine must have been broken since the material was presented so slowly. There was even the hint in his own voice that somehow he had magically caused the machine to slow down. The truth, though not quite so exciting, was nevertheless impressive. Jerry's practice and relaxation had resulted in improved control. His relaxation in the testing situation altered his perception—the machine had not changed but his ability to attend to information had.

There is very little difference between a hypnotic-induction technique and a self-hypnotic induction. As mentioned earlier, there are a great many different ways to induce hypnosis. The one presented here has been used successfully with a great many people and will probably work for you. Before presenting the actual procedure, however, we would like to make several points.

First, we will ask you to put the procedure on tape and to listen to the tape in order to experience what it is like to be hypnotized.

Because hypnosis has different meanings for different people, we will not make any other suggestions to you. Before using hypnosis as a vehicle for treating particular problems, you should consult with an expert who can help you identify some self-suggestions that are appropriate to your particular problem.

There are very general suggestions you can give such as "You will feel good, relaxed, and refreshed when you wake up." These should be used until you know how you will respond to more specific suggestions. This is particularly true if you want to use hypnosis for pain reduction or weight loss. You must make sure any changes in diet or eating habits will not damage your health. Likewise the pain you want to avoid might be providing a needed warning for you. You could have some problem requiring medical treatment, or the pain could serve to keep you from engaging in an activity that might injure you.

Remember, as you go through these procedures, hypnosis is a cooperative enterprise. If you are willing to allow yourself to go along with the suggestions and react passively to any distractions or interruptions, you will be able to experience what it is like to be hypnotized. This procedure will differ from what a hypnotist might do only in that it can't be paced to your responses. There will be times when you are responding to suggestions almost before they are made. There will be other times when you have not yet responded, and we ask you to move on. Either is acceptable, and you should react to these in a passive way. Okay, now sit back and relax!

Sit down in a comfortable chair with your feet flat on the floor. Let your hands rest comfortably either on the arms of the chair or in your lap. Now position your right hand so that you can fix your gaze on your right thumb nail. I will refer to your thumb nail as "the spot." I want you to stare fixedly at the spot while I talk to you. You can be hypnotized if you want to be. All that you need do is attend to the things that I ask.

If your mind occasionally wanders, just bring it back to the sound of my voice. Hypnosis involves your cooperation. There is nothing mystical or magical about it. By carefully directing your thoughts in the ways I suggest you can experience many amazing things. No matter how deeply hypnotized you become, you will always be able to hear the sound of my voice.

As you stare at the spot I want you to relax your entire body... Relax your arms... Breathe deeply and slowly... deeply and slowly. That's fine ... now relax your legs... Just completely relax, always able to hear the sound of my voice...

Continue to stare at the spot and as you do, relax the muscles in your face ... in your forehead ... and in your jaw. Let your mouth open slightly as you completely relax.

As you stare at the spot you may find your eyes becoming strained and tired. In a little while they will become very tired... It will be very hard to keep them open ... and finally they will close. When this happens you will be able to relax *completely*...

Continue to stare at the spot. As you do you may begin to notice certain things. Perhaps it becomes blurry and fuzzy as your eyes tire from the strain... You may see the colors under the nail change as the blood rushes into your finger with each pulse beat. Notice that as you relax, you are becoming very comfortable . . . deeply relaxed. It will be so nice when you can just close your eyes and let yourself go. . .

Your entire body is relaxed and your eyes are very tired from the strain of staring at the spot for so long. . . Your eyes are tired . . . and heavy. . . Tired . . . and heavy. . . It will be so nice when they close . . . almost on their own . . . and you can completely relax . . . and become deeply hypnotized. . .

If your eyes are already closed, that's fine . . . just completely relax. . . If they are not closed they soon will . . . just continue to stare at the spot a little longer. . . Your eyes are tired . . . and heavy. . . It is so hard to keep them open . . . such a strain . . . Soon you will have strained enough and they will close. . . Your eyes are so very tired . . . and heavy. . . If they have not yet closed on their own they soon will. . . Close them now. . . Close them now . . . Now you can completely relax and experience what it is like to be deeply hypnotized.

In a moment I am going to count from 1 to 20. With each count you will become more deeply hypnotized. . . With each count you will become more deeply hypnotized. . . No matter how deeply hypnotized you become you will always be able to hear the things that I say. . .

One . . . deeper . . . deeper . . . deeper. Relaxing all of the muscles in your arms and legs . . . in your entire body. Two . . . with each count drifting down into a pleasant deeply hypnotized state. Three . . . Four . . . Five . . . more and more relaxed . . . more deeply asleep. . . Six . . . down . . . deeper and deeper. . . Seven. . . Eight . . .

completely relaxed ... very comfortable ... enjoying the pleasant sensations... Nine ... Ten ... halfway down drifting deeper ... deeper ... still deeper... Eleven... Twelve... Thirteen ... deep asleep ... very relaxed ... and very comfortable... Fourteen... Fifteen ... down ... deeper ... and deeper asleep ... always able to hear my voice... Sixteen... Seventeen... Eighteen ... down ... completely relaxed ... at peace... Nineteen ... Twenty... *Deep asleep!*

Just continue to relax completely, enjoying the pleasant sensations of deep hypnosis...

In a moment I am going to wake you up. When I do, you will feel rested and refreshed... You will look forward to the rest of your day and you will remember everything that goes on.

You will find that when you want to you can induce a hypnotic state in yourself... You will do this by finding a comfortable chair, sitting down, closing your eyes and taking yourself through these procedures... You will always be in control and you will always be aware of your surroundings. You will not enter a hypnotic state unless you want to, and unless you consciously attempt it. You will be able to wake up at a moment's notice by simply counting to three. On the count of one you will take a deep breath. On the count of two you will stretch your arms and legs. On the count of three you will open your eyes and be wide awake.

That's fine... Now I am going to count from ten to one. With each count you will find yourself becoming more and more awake. By the time I reach one your eyes will be open and you will be wide awake, feeling rested and refreshed. . .

Ten. . . Nine. . . Eight. . . Seven. . . Six. . . waking up. . . Five . . . halfway there, more and more awake. . . Four . . . beginning to move around. . . Three . . . taking a deep breath. . . Two . . . stretching your arms and legs. . . One . . . *Eyes open! . . . Wide awake! Wide awake!*

9

Cognitive Behavior Modification

Donald Michenbaum, a psychologist at the University of Waterloo in Canada, offers yet another set of mental procedures. These, which he has labeled Cognitive Behavior Modification, are a sophisticated combination of the power of positive thinking and mental rehearsal.

There has been a fair amount of research that indicates our behavior is indeed shaped by what we think about ourselves. We mentioned earlier the differences between the inner dialogue of a winner and a loser, but the point is important enough to bear repeating. Let's take our winner and loser and put them both in the same speech-making situation.

The winner gives an interesting talk and gets applause as well as questions at the end. The loser is greeted by embarrassed silence. His presentation has been awkward and confusing, and both he and the audience could hardly wait for it to be over. As people leave the room they look at their feet to avoid catching the loser's eye. If they did they would feel compelled to say something about the speech. They know that they would either have to lie about how interesting it was, or they would have to tell him it was awful. They are too polite to do the latter, but their mute behavior does it for them.

Now Mr. Interviewer asks the two speakers to describe what was going on inside their heads as they presented the speech.

Mr. Loser says, "Well, I was worried about the speech when I was first asked to give it. I didn't think that what I had to say would be of any interest or relevance to them. I am sure they could have had a hundred other speakers who would have more to say. As I heard myself being introduced, I was thinking how dumb I was to let myself get into the situation to begin with. I noticed my hand was shaking and hoped that the audience wouldn't see this. When they didn't quiet down for the introduction I was convinced that they weren't interested in what I had to say. At that point I would have walked out if I could have.

"I tried to settle down and noticed that my voice cracked. Then I spotted the guy in the front row going to sleep. People seemed more interested in him than in me. With all of these distractions, I found I kept losing my place and repeating things. I'm sure what I said was confusing; I know *I* wasn't following it."

Mr. Winner responds a bit differently; "I was looking forward to the speech. I knew the topic would be of interest to the audience, and I anticipated a lot of give and take. I figured that they were lucky to have asked me to be a speaker since I can be entertaining and know more about the topic than anyone in this area.

"I was amused when the person introducing me was unable to get the attention of the entire group. He obviously needed practice. Actually, I like it better that way because it gives me a chance to assert myself and take control right from the beginning. When I stood up I knew I was ready. I could feel my heart beat a little more quickly and my hands had a slight tremor, a sign that means I'm ready.

"As I began, I noticed that one of the men in the front row had gone to sleep. I thought that it must have been a tough night for him. With the dinner and all the drinking. I would have let him sleep but figured he would be upset if he missed what I had to say, so I asked the people next to him to wake him up."

The words express the different perceptions and feelings of winners and losers. Dr. Michenbaum would have you change the words, but would go a little farther in utilizing some of the theories about human learning.

For both behavior and attitude to change it is necessary that you: 1) have the appropriate behavior available; 2) recognize when you are engaging in inappropriate or counter-productive behavior; 3) be motivated to change; 4) be positively reinforced for any change.

Cognitive behavior modification procedures attempt to incorporate all of the points just mentioned. They are fairly effective with some difficult problems as well as being useful in controlling impulsive behavior. Some of Dr. Michenbaum's earlier research focused on just such a problem. He worked with hyperactive children and found that by modifying what they said to themselves he could get them to gain control over their tendency to jump from one task to another without completing them.

In effect, he could get them to improve their attention span and stay with a project, thereby dramatically reducing their disruptive behavior. What he had to do to accomplish this goal was first to make the children aware of when they *were* jumping. Then he taught them simple self-instructional phrases such as "no, slow down!" He had them employ these both aloud and silently and provided rewards every time they practiced the procedure.

In essence what Dr. Michenbaum did with hyperactive children is what you would do with yourself, particularly in those situations where physical symptoms are not problems but rather new attitudes are the things that need to be developed. Theoretically, the task is simpler with a cooperative adult who already recognizes a problem and is self-motivated to change it. Under these circumstances you sensitize yourself to the negative self-statements and instead identify positive ones you can make that tend to re-interpret the situation, thus building your confidence and self-esteem.

Because external motivations can be used, (for example you could reward a child with candy or money every time he or she used a self-control statement) cognitive behavior modification is often very helpful in working with children and with more severe problems such as hyperactivity.

As we mentioned earlier, there can be a problem if you tend to be caught up in self-instruction during the actual task, particularly if the task you want to accomplish is a complex or difficult one. A child can say "now, slow down" as he gets up to race across the room. It is a simple command to stop a simple behavior. Giving a speech is very complex and too many corrections during the actual speech will detract from performance. It is because of this that the procedures are best used to enhance self-esteem and confidence before the actual performance.

One point to bear in mind is that these procedures allow you to experience anxiety. With the procedures in Part I, a major goal is the reduction or removal of feelings of physiological arousal. In the cognitive behavior modification example these feelings were accepted and simply reinterpreted in a more adaptive way such as "my shaky hands mean I am ready."

When physical symptoms are not very important but

anxiety is, and when more adaptive behaviors need to be developed, cognitive behavior modification can be a very useful procedure. Jim, age 37, is a case in point.

Jim was one of those fortunate people who had been spared having to deal with any kind of major illness either with himself or his family. Everyone had been healthy, or else they had died rather suddenly. He didn't remember his grandmother. His grandfather had died of a heart attack. And he had a couple of friends who had died in accidents.

Within his family, illness was something to be avoided at all costs, and the family had been remarkably successful. Jim attributed this to good health care and common sense. The family regularly went for medical and dental checks, and at the first sign of a cold, everything took a back seat to its treatment.

Things changed abruptly for Jim when one of his employees, a young man of 27, went for a physical and was told that he had a fatal disease.

At about this same time Jim's mother-in-law had a stroke, and both he and his wife found themselves feeling responsible for taking care of her. Her husband had died some years earlier, and the other children were neither mature enough nor financially able to handle this difficult task.

Never having had to deal with illness before, Jim was at a loss as to how to respond. He found himself feeling worthless and was very concerned about how his behavior must be affecting the people around him. Like the audience in the example of Mr. Loser's speech, Jim found that he could neither look his mother-in-law nor his co-worker in the eye, let alone talk to them.

He found himself morbidly curious on the one hand and outraged that he should feel this way on the other. He wanted to offer some support and assistance but didn't know how, and he convinced himself that any attempts on his part would be misconstrued to mean that he didn't really know how they felt. In the case of his employee he knew he should conduct business as usual but found he couldn't.

Cognitive behavior modification was used because Jim needed to modify the attitudes he had, both toward himself and those who were sick. In addition, his own anxiety was beginning to interfere with his ability to determine more appropriate ways to respond.

The situation that was most immediately important was the one at work, especially since his own productivity had tapered off to such a degree that his job was in jeopardy. With this in mind, Jim was asked to describe what his thoughts and feelings would be when he had to interact with his employee. He described the following inner dialogue around a situation in which he needed to ask the worker to run some checks on potential customers.

"Gee, I hate to give him this job, but I can't find anyone else. I wonder how he feels. He hasn't talked much about the illness. I can't ask; he'll think I'm implying that he's not doing the work. Yeah, but if I don't ask he'll think I don't care.

"His face is a little yellow, and his mouth looks funny. I wonder if that's the medication. I have to stop staring. Maybe I could tell a joke. No, I'm not good at that, and he'd probably take it the wrong way. I wish he would take time off. Damn it, why does he put me in this position."

Using Jim's dialogue, it was easy to point out how he was second-guessing everything he did. In addition, he was shown how he was assuming all of the responsibility for his employee, and how he was trying to make all the decisions without asking the most important person for input.

Jim was helped to develop a new inner dialogue that allowed him to express directly his concern for his employee, and at the same time allow him to ask for advice regarding the best way to handle the situation. In treatment he explored various ways of saying things and rehearsed these in role-playing situations. He was reinforced in his efforts by the responses of the therapist who was playing the part of the co-worker. Within a couple of sessions, Jim had developed enough confidence and had convinced himself of the need to confront the issues directly, so that he was able to engage in a productive discussion with the sick man.

He returned to report that the employee had been very appreciative of the interest, and had in fact been concerned about Jim. He had noticed Jim's difficulty and wanted to do something to put him at ease but didn't know how.

Another area in which cognitive behavior modification has been applied successfully is in modifying what individuals say to themselves in social situations.

Mark was 26 years old and had a long history of difficulty when it came to developing relationships with the opposite sex. He became so anxious at the thought of a face-to-face encounter with a girl that he had become the butt of many jokes. His situation had not been helped by the fact that in high school he had been cruelly teased by boys and girls alike. Small wonder that his self-confidence in social situations was at such a low point. He was Jerry Lewis and Woody Allen rolled into one, but minus the personality and talent.

If someone he knew came up and initiated a conversation he could be both interesting and funny. But let him have to make the first move, or have that person be a stranger, and he would make more blunders than the Three Stooges.

His behavior at parties was legendary. On one occasion a girl he was standing near had asked him a question just as he was drinking some punch. He choked on the punch, coughing some on the girl, who was sitting down. Very upset and embarrassed, he had reached to wipe it off and had spilled the entire glass in her lap. She jumped up, and he stepped on her foot. Then, while still standing on her foot, he had bumped into her, knocking her flat on her back.

Such failures, piled one on top of the other, led to feelings of worthlessness and to social isolation. He was afraid to go out and even try to get involved. The biggest problem was that he couldn't live with his loneliness. He needed to be loved and needed someone to love.

The tremendous need for involvement was part of his problem, and this became clear when he was asked to describe what would go on in his head when he was about to approach a girl. A large number of the thoughts were aimed at the distant future. Before even being introduced to the girl he was thinking ahead to where the relationship might go. He was so concerned that he wouldn't be liked, that a dating relationship wouldn't develop, that they wouldn't be married, that he lost sight of the fact that all he was doing was saying hello. He would go over and become so overloaded by his own anxieties, past failures, and predictions of future failures that he would be unable to speak.

The first step in treatment was to get him to focus on taking one small step in developing social skills. Mark learned that he had to stop looking toward the future, and that all that was needed was for him to be able to say hello without falling apart. This was the goal. (We might emphasize here that goal-setting such as this will be critical for you in any self-help program. Don't try to bite off more than you can chew.)

Once Mark was able to narrow his focus, it became a simple matter to identify his negative self-statements and to modify them. After all, he had not failed (in his own mind) in the past in just saying hello. He had failed to develop this fantastic relationship and to be the world's greatest lover. By recognizing this it was possible to give him the confidence he needed to start modifying his behavior and cognitions.

Over a period of several months, meeting on a weekly basis, it was possible to get Mark to develop a dating relationship with a girl he had known for quite some time. At last report things were progressing nicely.

Cognitive behavior modification procedures can be fairly straightforward and simple, or very complex. Sticking with the simpler applications, we are going to give you a few suggestions that you can easily employ.

Remember that the key to cognitive behavior modification involves the following: First, you must be motivated to see what it is that you are doing wrong. The focus here is on identifying the negative thoughts and feelings you have that tend to lower your self-esteem and interfere with your performance.

As soon as you become aware of what it is that you are doing wrong, you'll need to identify alternative cognitions or thoughts. The secret is to find things to say, think, and do that will facilitate positive feelings toward yourself while also improving your performance. Performance improvement is important because that success, particularly in a self-control program, will supply the necessary reinforcement to help you maintain a change for the better.

Step I

Pick a specific situation that you remember feeling uncomfortable in, one where you found yourself doubting your own ability and wanted to improve. Common problems are giving a speech, taking a test, meeting new people, disciplining your children, or trying to make a sale.

Step II

Get out a pad and pencil and write down everything you can remember about the particular incident. Start by thinking about the day before the event occurred. See if you can remember any thoughts or feelings you might have had at that time about the upcoming event; then write them all down.

Moving to the day of the event. Try to recall what you were thinking and feeling at the following times, and write these down.

1. As you were getting ready to leave to do whatever it was that you were involved with.
2. As you were arriving. What were you feeling? Any muscle tension, stomach sensations, etc. What were you thinking? Describe what you saw and what your reactions were. Who was there? What did they look like? What was the physical setting like and how did it affect you?
3. As you began to get involved, made your presentation, etc. What were you feeling and thinking; how were people reacting, and how did that affect you?
4. What happened during the event? What were your thoughts and feelings? Record every detail.
5. How did you feel at the end? What were other people's reactions?

Look at your descriptions and identify and underline all of the negative thoughts, derogatory self-references, etc.

Step III

Find an individual who you feel is capable of doing those things you want to do. Ask him to go over your experience with you and help you alter your thoughts. For example, get him to tell you what his thoughts and reactions would be under similar situations. How would he interpret the behavior of the audience.

Don't feel that you have to take his words as the gospel. Use his ideas to find your own things to say to yourself. The important thing is to make positive, helpful statements. You may want to refer back to Chaper XI for some examples.

Step IV

Take the new, positive description of the event that you come up with and put it on tape. Then relax as you listen to the tape and try to create the scene vividly that you are describing while also rehearsing all of the positive statements and attitudes.

Part Four:

HOW TO USE COMBINED PROCEDURES

In the previous chapters we turned our attention to those procedures that tended to focus in on either physical or emotional symptoms associated with stress. In the next three chapters we will be dealing with procedures that bridge this gap between physical and cognitive methodologies.

There are a large number of problems and situations where some combination of procedures is desirable. For example, there are many physical problems that are aggravated by stress. These include ulcers, hypertension, vascular and tension headaches, circulatory problems, arthritis, muscle aches and pains of various types. More often than not, in addition to the physical problem, we find our emotions equally affected, particularly if the problem is a chronic one. It is difficult to live with an illness for months or years and not have it affect your attitude and involvement with life.

When this happens it is possible to mix and match procedures in order to design a program to fit your own special needs. It is important to remember that even when a single procedure is involved in treatment, it is almost always modified in some way so as to be effective for both emotional and physical reactions to stress. The primary emphasis may be in one direction or the other, but both are invariably affected.

10

Systematic Desensitization and Implosion

Systematic desensitization is based on the fact that it is impossible to be physically relaxed and anxious at the same time. Specifically designed for the treatment of fears or phobias, it has been applied to changing both attitudes and feelings, as well as to changing behavior. Some of the fears that have been treated include those associated with flying, snakes, dogs, tests, giving speeches, and even surgery. In fact, it is possible to use the procedure to help cope with any fear that can be defined in terms of specific situations or conditions.

As a procedure for treating anxiety and fear, systematic desensitization has been very successful. Usually only 6 to 14 sessions of about one hour each are required, and therapists who have used the procedures report improvement in 70 to 90 percent of their cases. Costs for treatment are similar to those for other forms of psychotherapy, ranging from $25 per session to upward of $70.

To illustrate the application of the procedures, try to imagine that you are afraid of the dark. When you are left alone in a dark place you become panicked, your heart races, you begin to perspire, breathing becomes more rapid, and you feel like running and screaming. You aren't sure what is so frightening, only that as soon as the lights go out, especially when you are alone, you always feel this fear.

It may have been strong enough that it has actually interfered with your enjoyment of life. You can't go to sleep at night without a light being on. The thought of camping or walking alone is out of the question. You didn't vacation with the kids because you didn't want to explore the caves. You have stocked up on flashlights and candles in case of a power failure. Even driving at night is something to be avoided. You don't really feel safe after sunset unless you're sitting in the well-lighted living room of your own house.

Finally you've had enough of this fear and decide to get some help. You've heard about systematic desensitization, go to the therapist, and the first thing he does is teach you a progressive relaxation procedure similar to the one presented in Part I. He explains to you that your body cannot be both relaxed and anxious at the same time. What he is going to do once you have learned to relax is gradually to increase your exposure to your own fear. To do this he asks you to make a list of situations directly related to your fear of the dark. The list should proceed from that situation which is least anxiety-inducing, to one that would completely "freak you out."

Together you work out descriptions for eight or ten different situations. The result might look something like the following:

1. Thinking about nightfall.
2. Seeing a children's book with pictures and a story about the dark.
3. Looking outside after it is dark while inside my own house.

4. Noticing the lights flicker.
5. Thinking about a power shortage.
6. Driving alone at night.
7. Having a mechanical breakdown on a lonely road at night.
8. Being completely alone and trapped in a totally black place with no way to escape.

As soon as you have learned to use the progressive relaxation procedures, your therapist begins systematically exposing you to the situations. You close your eyes in a quiet room and relax. You then are asked to visualize the first item in your list. It is described very carefully, and you are asked to rehearse it and to try to create as vivid an image as you can. If you feel your anxiety beginning to rise, you signal the therapist and he stops presenting the scene. You relax and start again. Gradually over the 6 to 16 sessions you are able to visualize all of the scenes without becoming anxious.

It has been found that this kind of program will result in actual behavior change. For example, people who are afraid of dogs have been able to overcome their fear in the treatment room so that they were able to go out and pet dogs, something they couldn't do before. The same is true of performance anxiety. The success in an imaginary situation in the laboratory can be generalized so that you can be successful in the real situation.

One way to make this transition easier is to develop an *in vivo* desensitization program. In the case of fear of the dark, this would involve actually exposing you to darkness rather than just talking about it. This would be a fairly easy fear to work on, since all that would be required would be gradually reducing the illumination of the room. Others, however, are hard to create at home or in a therapist's office. When this is the case the more standard procedure is used.

As you can see from the presentation, systematic desensitization combines relaxation and rehearsal. It can be further modified so that any of the procedures in Part I could also be used for relaxation. One procedure, biofeedback, has been found to be especially useful for several reasons.

As you learn to relax using biofeedback, there is an objective ongoing indication of your success. By leaving you attached to the equipment when items on the list are being presented, it is possible to watch the meter to see if you are getting anxious. Often the equipment is more sensitive to increases in anxiety than you can be. A modification such as this in the desensitization procedure can be important, especially if it is easier for you to place confidence in the equipment than in yourself.

While we are on the subject of systematic desensitization we might also deal with a procedure called implosion. Whereas systematic desensitization attempts to reduce your anxiety gently, implosion is designed to overload you. The procedure really emphasizes that you have nothing to fear but fear itself.

Use the desensitization procedure but remove the relaxation training and just rehearse the last, most frightening item on the list you made. You have an example of implosion. Presumably, if you are vividly confronted by the worst aspects of your fear and survive them, no basis remains for the fear and it goes away.

The classic scene of the Marine drill instructor, nose to nose with the young recruit, yelling and screaming to get his orders across is the perfect example of a flooding experience. In implosion the therapist is the drill instructor.

Unfortunately, many training programs seem based on the model, including much of graduate education.

The master illusionist and escape artist, The Amazing Randi, chose to use the concept of implosion in quite a different way. In order to overcome his fear of people he forced himself to get up on stage to perform his feats of prestidigitation, knowing full well that if he confronted his fear in this way he would have to succeed.

Another example of implosion, where one paints a mental image and begins to describe a scene as it might take place, could be the case of the businessman who is afraid to go in and ask his boss for a raise. Implosion in this instance would have the man imagining the worst possible scene, beginning outside the boss's office.

He's made up his mind that he deserves a raise after assuming new responsibilities. The time has come to take the initiative and ask the boss face-to-face for more money. The conversation and events could go something like this. . . .

Imagine that as you walk into the boss's office you find yourself feeling a bit apprehensive. You even notice that your stomach is starting to rumble; your palms are sweaty; you're getting more and more upset; and you're feeling increasingly warm the further into the office you get. You walk over to the boss, and he doesn't even look up from his desk. He grunts a brief acknowledgement that he knows you're there and goes right on with his work. There you are, feeling dwarfed by the huge mahogany desk, when suddenly your boss looks up and says,

"What do *you* want, Lowell!"

"Well, sir I'd like to talk to you about, uhm, my salary . . ."

"*Your salary?*"

"Yes sir, I've been working for the company for a long time now and I . . . I think that the changes in the cost of living and the increased responsibility I have, uhm, justify a raise."

"I'm glad you brought that up. I've been meaning to have an appraisal conference with you, and you've saved me the trouble. Who are you kidding? Costs have gone up. Do you think my profits are also increasing? As it is, you aren't worth what you're being paid, and you have the gall to come in here and ask for a raise! That report you turned in last week. . . I had to go over it myself because you didn't do your job. You have the audacity to ask for more money . . . Well, I'll tell you something, Lowell, I'm going to cut your salary by 10 percent. I ought to fire you, but I feel sorry for your family and don't want to add to the burden that you cause them. Now get out of this office!"

An extreme situation yes! But the purpose of implosion is to exaggerate to the extreme, beyond whatever *could* happen. By doing this an individual is overwhelmed by his own feelings and insecurities to such a degree that usually the experience in therapy is far more frightening than reality could ever be.

Is implosion an option for you? In our lives we all seem to go through many trials by fire. The coach or parent who tells you to get up and do it again after you have been hurt or knocked down, is employing a mini-version of this. If you survived those demands and came through, then you may profit from implosion. If instead, you found yourself driven farther away, dropping the sport or withdrawing, then implosion may not be useful.

In the case histories that follow we emphasize systematic desensitization, both because it is a more common form of treatment, and because implosive scenes are only too easy for most of us to construct.

Susan was 17, a junior in high school. She came from an upper-middle-class family that placed a great deal of emphasis on education, both as a means to a career and also as a preparation for a full life. Thus it was very important to them that Susan do well in high school. This was necessary in order to get into a "good" college and be exposed to the "right" experiences and people. Susan's parents would have been upset to be told that they were viewing college as a supermarket for appropriate son-in-laws. However, in spite of their denials, this was a major factor in determining the amount of pressure they put on their daughter to obtain good grades.

Susan was absolutely everything her parents could want her to be, with one possible exception. She was attractive, well-mannered, loving, concerned about other people and very responsible. What she was not was a scholar. Susan was a "C" student, and she knew it. Her parents recognized their daughter's mediocrity when it came to grades only too well. They accepted it and consoled her when she would cry because she had studied so hard and had only gotten a "C" while her brother, without studying, would get "A's." They would explain that they understood, but somehow their own pressure was always there for her to do better and to study harder. Their disappointment was obvious to Susan, and it hurt her.

Because she was so responsible Susan studied harder than the other students. Her parents helped quiz her before tests until she knew the material. But somehow, by the time she got to school, her anxiety over the examination would reach such a point that her mind would be a blank. Half the time she would leave not knowing what she had put on the test paper.

Systematic desensitization was chosen as Susan's treatment approach for several reasons. First, it was primarily anxiety, not physical symptoms, that was getting in her way in test situations. In addition, a discussion of her study habits and her method of taking tests revealed that she knew and used adequate measures to insure the possibility of better grades. She did not need to learn new techniques— all she had to do was lower her anxiety enough to show what she already knew.

Susan described her anxiety as building rather suddenly. Usually she would feel fine the night before a test and while walking to school on the day of the exam. Even a few minutes before the test she would still be fairly calm. Once inside the classroom, as she sat down, she would begin to notice some anxiety. She would find her hands sweating so much she was constantly wiping them off. Her breathing would increase, and she could feel her heart beating. These reactions would increase as the test materials were being passed out.

For Susan there was a big jump from controllable anxiety as the test was being passed out to uncontrollable panic as she looked at the first question. Up to this point she had been reminding herself of answers to questions that she was sure would be asked. Then, as she looked at the first item her mind would go blank. She would tell herself it was silly to move to another question but would go over the test looking for anything she could answer. Unfortunately, she could not stop on any question long enough, nor control her racing thoughts, to come up with a correct answer. After the exam she could sit down and think of answers, but that was too late.

With systematic desensitization a list of anxiety-arousing items was constructed, beginning with the night before the test:

1. Reading material you think will be covered on the test.

2. Being quizzed by your parents.
3. Walking to school and rehearsing the material.
4. Talking with friends outside the class.
5. Sitting in your seat and getting ready.
6. Receiving your test.
7. Realizing that the test is important to college admission.
8. Not knowing the answer to the first questions.

Susan was able to go over the items in a fairly short time (six sessions). The relaxation procedures she was to learn were also put on tape for her to take home and listen to. This outside structure provided some additional support and confidence for her. After going through the items and learning the relaxation procedures, Susan found that she was able to use the relaxation training exercises to gain enough control in actual testing situations to avoid panic, and her marks moved up to B's and occasional A's.

The second case we are going to present involves another example of performance anxiety. Evelyn is a professional musician who plays the flute and should have been first chair in the symphony of a large city. She could play anything with fantastic control when she was alone or with friends, but in concert, though her playing was still good, it wasn't the same. Her anxiety took just enough off that she found herself playing behind other musicians who had far less talent and ability than she did.

Having an artist's temperament to begin with, the frustration of taking a back seat to her colleagues would often cause her to fly into a rage. On these occasions her hysterical outbursts would rival those of Elizabeth Taylor in *Who's Afraid of Virginia Woolf.* Often these tantrums were aimed at the wrong people—innocent bystanders. It wasn't until she began losing friends, and when her lover threatened to walk out, that she decided to get some help.

Systematic desensitization was used with Evelyn, but the program took longer than it might have. Her rage at other people kept her focused on them and impeded her accepting and dealing with her own inadequacy at functioning under pressure. The first few sessions were spent getting through enough of the rage so that the problem could be recognized and treated. Once this occurred, progress was rapid, and Evelyn was able to give the best sustained performances of her life. The result was that she is now first-chair flutist in the symphony.

A major part of systematic desensitization involves learning to relax. Presumably you have learned this from the procedures that have already been presented. What we will do here is give you an outline of the procedures that are followed in the laboratory. These should provide you with an idea of how long your own program is likely to take and what should be involved in each session.

Rarely do we exceed 10 sessions in treating someone with Systematic Desensitization. This is particularly true when the fear is related to a real performance situation. For example, when we desensitize a person for giving speeches, performing in front of an audience, or taking a test.

We would recommend that if you are going to engage in a self-treatment approach you spread the sessions out so that you have two per week. Placing them more closely together won't give you time to assimilate everything and to develop the necessary relaxation. Putting them farther apart will dilute the experience too much.

Step I

We attempt to accomplish two things. The first is to take a history of the problem. This is done in the first treatment session and provides the basis for developing the eight-item hierarchy of fear-related items. We also begin training in progressive relaxation in the first session. In session two, usually two to three days after session one, we ask the subject how relaxation is progressing and work with them to develop the hierarchy further.

The exact number of items is not critical, but you need to describe them well enough that you can develop good visual images.

Step II

We almost invariably start presentation of the items on the hierarchy in session three. These are the least threatening (starting at the top of the list and not covering more than two new items per session). So even if you are still learning the procedures you have enough skill to begin.

In session three we present item one and ask you to visualize it, stopping the presentation if you feel any anxiety. As soon as we can make it through the item without an appreciable difference in your anxiety, we move to item two. As mentioned above, we do not go through more than two items per session even if you report no anxiety. We also present each item twice in each session.

Between each item you are given time to relax again. In the subsequent session other items are tackled. Thus a record of what happened across sessions might look like this.

Session 3: Item one and two presented. Item two generated anxiety.
Session 4: Item one presented. Item two presented.

Item three presented. Successfully made it through item three.

Session 5:   Item three presented. Item four presented, but not completed.

Session 6:   Item three, four, and five completed.

Session 7:   Item five, six, and seven presented.

Session 8:   Item seven and eight presented.

Session 9:   Item seven and eight presented. Therapy terminated.

11

Hypnosis

The second procedure that we have included under the heading of combined approaches is hypnosis. In use for a long time, and with a broad clinical application, hypnosis is difficult to include under any of the approaches we have talked about previously. Its flexibility makes it better suited to be presented under the heading of combined approaches.

Modern hypnosis dates back to a man called Mesmer who lived in France during the 1700s. He is credited with many of the medical and psychological applications of this technique, and his influence was so great that for many years hypnosis was referred to as Mesmerism.

The application of hypnosis to stress-related problems has been broad indeed. Sometimes hypnotists induce a trance state and then simply make very direct suggestions that are designed to alter or remove both physical and psychological symptoms. Statements like "you will feel no more pain," "you will be happy," "you will feel rested," "you will forget," "you will remember," are enough to, in good hypnotic subjects, change physical or emotional feelings.

Direct suggestions like the ones mentioned have been

used to remove warts and blisters; cure skin rashes; reduce or eliminate the pain of childbirth, dentistry, and surgery; and eliminate fears.

Hypnotic suggestions can be simple, but they also can be extremely complex. Many psychoanalytically oriented therapists have used hypnosis as a tool. By inducing a hypnotic state in patients they can relax them enough to help them recover hidden fears, lost memories, and unresolved conflicts. This type of work is best left in the hands of an expert and is mentioned only to help you understand the truly broad application of hypnosis.

One use of hypnosis during and after World War II was as a technique to help veterans recover from emotional problems resulting from repressed memories. Occasionally the pressures of battle and death became too much for an individual and caused him to break down. He would develop symptoms that, analysts believed, would not go away until he recovered the repressed memory that caused the problem. Through hypnosis the individual can be made to relive the trauma and go through a catharsis, usually resulting in a cure. In many ways the hypnotic experience is much like the implosion talked about in the last chapter.

Part of the merit of hypnosis, however, is the alluring mystical aspects of the procedure. Our preconceived notions about it serve as a distraction from the problem that is troubling us. The hypnotic state itself has so much pull that it overshadows our anxiety. It can be used by a hypnotist to redirect our attention in more productive and stress-reducing ways.

There are many different ways one can be hypnotized, from the familiar swinging coin to the use of a strobe light. But the most important aspect of the induction procedure is that it should facilitate trust in the relationship between the subject and the hypnotist. In order to be effective, hypnosis has to be a cooperative venture built on mutual trust and understanding. As a subject you need to be in a receptive and fairly calm state of mind in order to be hypnotized. It is ideal if you are *mildly* interested although too much interest can be distracting.

Hypnosis is such a powerful tool it is too bad that not everyone is a good subject. In fact, approximately 10 percent of the population will not respond to any hypnotic suggestions. Another 10 percent of the population is so receptive that hypnotic states are very easily induced. The remaining 80 percent of the population falls somewhere in between these two extremes. There have been a great many claims as to what makes a good hypnotic subject, but none of them have been proven scientifically. The best way to find out for yourself is to be hypnotized.

Since your willingness to be hypnotized plays such an important role in the effectiveness of hypnosis as a tool, it can be very helpful if you are already in a positive frame of mind before you begin.

A well-publicized example of hypnosis is the case of Ken Norton in his first fight with Muhammad Ali. Much was made of the fact that Norton was going to be hypnotized before the fight. The fact that he broke Ali's jaw and won the fight lent much credence to the procedure, especially considering the relative obscurity of Norton's talents as a prize fighter. Interestingly, the next time Norton faced Ali he did so without the help of hypnosis and wound up losing the fight. Is it fair to assume that hypnosis played a factor in his winning the first fight, and the absence of it aided in his losing the second fight?

Well, it is generally accepted that hypnosis allows people to do certain things without necessarily giving them *added* power or support to excel in a particular situation. It is a tool that facilitates an increased level of self-control but doesn't offer increased physical skills. If you don't have the strength to lift an automobile when you're not hypnotized, you won't suddenly become the strongest human in the world. What it can do is relax you and help you focus your attention to such a point that your innate abilities and talents are maximized.

Hence, Ken Norton may have been given extra powers of self-control and more confidence in his own abilities. He was able to fight his fight, not Ali's, and aggressively sought out his opponent in a rather fixed and strategically planned way. In the second fight, however, it seemed as if Norton was guided more by his emotions to *beat* Ali and prove that the first fight wasn't a fluke. This increased pressure, if it existed, could have resulted in Norton losing his cool to Ali's showboating style.

Let's move from speculation about Ken Norton to some known facts about hypnosis. To understand the inner workings of hypnosis it may be helpful to look at the three phases involved in the procedure. The first is the "hypnotic induction," which is nothing more than a series of suggestions that are aimed at eliciting an individual's cooperation, while also directing his attention and thoughts toward a more relaxed and calm state.

The induction can be accomplished in a number of ways. If the hypnotist is sensitive to an individual's needs a procedure will be selected and used which responds to these expectations. Thus, if you are expecting some kind of mystical experience, the hypnotist may tell you how hypnosis has been used in age regression to get people to relive earlier times. He may talk about the use of hypnosis to explore past lives or to try and substantiate ESP or reincarnation. He may use an induction technique that causes you to gaze at an eye or a spinning wheel.

On the other hand, if the hypnotist perceives that you are

more interested in the scientific aspects of hypnosis he may talk about clinical applications of the procedure in pain reduction. He may speak about it as a tool for facilitating relaxation and may suggest that because hypnosis is a relaxed state, it is associated with increases in alpha production. He may then say that by having you stare at a strobe light it is possible to drive your brain's electrical activity and to create an alpha state.

Thus your orientation and expectations should influence selection of an induction procedure. Whether the hypnotist is sensitive to your needs or not, what you experience as the induction proceeds will be very much associated with your expectations. For some people hypnosis is a state essentially no different from the waking state. They feel clearheaded and in complete control. They hear the hypnotist making suggestions and respond internally by thinking, "I can go along if I want to, I can also resist. I'm comfortable, so why fight it anyway, I wouldn't want to disappoint him."

A second type of experience might be a little less ordinary. Some subjects describe the state as about halfway between sleeping and waking—a little like taking a nap and hearing the phone ring. As it rings you hear it but aren't sure if it really happened or if you were dreaming.

A third type of response is less common but happens to some people. Their experience is one of almost complete dissociation from their body. They feel as if they were floating in clouds.

How you experience hypnosis will depend upon what you expect and on the extent to which you can allow your attention to become completely caught up in the hypnotist's suggestions. The more complete your concentration, the closer you are likely to come to the third example.

The second phase of hypnosis takes place after the induction procedure is completed and is commonly referred to as the trance. It is at this point that some specific suggestions can be made regarding improved performance or removal of symptoms associated with stress.

The last part of the procedure involves giving the subject post-hypnotic suggestions. Many of the problems we have do not occur while we are in the hypnotic state. We need to influence our perceptions and behavior at other times, and this is the function of post-hypnotic suggestions. As an example, you might be told that "the next time you go to the dentist you will find that as soon as you sit in his chair you will be very comfortable and relaxed."

The key to the effectiveness of post-hypnotic suggestions is that they not be general, but instead focus on a particular situation. Another important factor is the length of time between the suggestion and when it is to be effective. Ideally, a suggestion will be specific and deal with some situation that will soon be encountered. If these conditions are met, the suggestion is much more likely to be effective, and if it is effective the first time it will often continue to be so.

As an example, a general suggestion that you will lose weight or quit smoking is not likely to be too effective. If the suggestion is more specific such as "tonight after a few bites you will find you had enough to eat and will push the plate away," you will have better success. Control in this situation becomes a positive indication to you that you can gain the upper hand in other areas. As confidence increases so will your ability to deal with broader, more general conditions. This same information, by the way, is critical to suggestions you give yourself in a self-induced hypnotic state.

A case history that illustrates the results hypnosis can achieve, when properly utilized, is that of Mary, an aspiring musician in her junior year at college. A talented violin player, Mary had begun to complain about pain in her index finger, sometimes a dull throbbing, more often a shooting pain that greatly interfered with her performance.

Normally, if any of us were to feel a muscular pain we wouldn't be too concerned. We would figure that with proper rest it would subside; so we wouldn't be anxious. In Mary's case the pain didn't lessen, and she turned to her family internist, hoping to learn what the problem was and why she was suffering such acute sensations when she played her violin. The physician was unable to find a cause for the pain and prescribed Valium, thinking that this medication would at least relax her and alleviate some of the pressure she was feeling.

By now Mary had begun to reduce her practice time. This aggravated her anxiety because she was not keeping up with other students or her own expectancies. The Valium gave her a floating sensation she didn't like. She couldn't concentrate, and the pain remained.

Next Mary tried a dermatologist, thinking that possibly the sensation was a problem he could deal with. All he accomplished was to remove the callous on the end of her finger and a "particle" that somehow disappeared before Mary could see it. Unfortunately, the pain continued.

Mary consulted an orthopedist, who saw nothing wrong with the finger and felt that the problem was psychological rather than physical. He recommended a psychiatrist, and Mary went, since she was desperate and felt her future career was in danger. The psychiatrist asked about her childhood, and she walked out.

It was frustrating enough to have difficulty playing, but what was more disheartening was that music, with its central role in her life, suddenly was being threatened by some unknown malady that no doctor could even come close to curing. She turned to what she felt was her last alternative and contemplated the use of biofeedback, hoping this procedure would provide an answer.

After consultation it was suggested to Mary that although biofeedback was a useful procedure for pain related to muscle tension it did not seem adequate for her needs. Mary had been asked to keep records of when the pain occurred, how intense it was, what she was playing and what the position of her finger was. The records clearly indicated that muscle tension was not involved, which argued against the use of biofeedback in this particular instance. The therapist then took time to explain to Mary about the use of hypnotic suggestion for the reduction of pain. He gave her some reading to do and also some reassurance.

Because of the talking and the reading, Mary was able to develop a very positive attitude toward the use of hypnosis. She became an excellent subject, and direct suggestions were used to reduce the pain she was experiencing. Because Mary had kept such detailed records of practice time and pain, it was possible to determine exactly how much of a reduction there was in her pain, both in terms of frequency and intensity as well as duration. Following a single session the number of pains dropped from 7 per hour to less than 1. Mary was thus able to increase her practice time from one to four hours per day. In addition, the intensity of the pains was dramatically reduced so that they now felt more like legitimate sensations caused by the effort of her playing.

Hypnosis was helpful to Mary for several reasons. First, it got her involved with someone who was interested in her and willing to spend some time. Next, it provided an explanation and hope. The hypnotist was seen as a source of support, and the procedure promised her some immediate relief while reducing her fears about the consequences of continued loss of practice. Prior to treatment Mary had determined that she would have to drop out of school if something could not be done. Fortunately for Mary's future, this was not necessary.

Hypnosis does have a great many uses although it is not a panacea. The cautions that were presented in the self-hypnosis chapter apply here as well. For more information on hypnosis you might find *Hypnosis Fact and Fiction,* by F.L. Marcuse, a useful source book.

12

Application of Combined Procedures

In the next few pages we will present a number of different case histories that involve some stress-related problem and were chosen for several reasons.

First, we wanted to illustrate the diversity of problems that can be dealt with by the various treatments presented so far. We also wanted to underscore the flexibility of the different procedures and show how they can be combined in order to respond to special needs or situations. Finally, we hope we can strike a responsive cord in you. It has been our experience that the problems we are presenting are only too common. If you're like most of us you probably thought you were living in your own private hell. Well, welcome to the club. With a little confidence and discipline you can graduate to the status of alumni.

Marge was the 27-year-old mother of two very active daughters. The girls, four and five years old, were the apple of their father's eye. According to Marge's husband they could do no wrong; however, she knew differently.

Both parents were college graduates, Bill a successful aircraft company engineer and Marge a history major turned housewife. Although she had gotten a degree in education, Marge had married at the end of school and never really worked, except as a teacher's assistant.

Bill was one of those people who is never wrong. He took control of situations and was very quick to make decisions. If there was the least bit of hesitation on anyone else's part, he took charge. It was qualities such as these that Marge admired in her husband. She saw him as being very capable and strong, which was in sharp contrast to how she viewed herself.

Deep inside Marge was sure that being married was the best thing for her, since she doubted that she could support herself or function independently as a teacher. On the surface, however, Marge was a woman in conflict. She had a degree, and women friends keep reminding her that she was more than "just a housewife." She felt she should prove herself to her husband and friends; the only thing holding her back was that she was afraid of failure. As a result of the conflict she attempted to exert control over situations (especially with the children), had second thoughts continually about what she was doing, and failed to follow through on most projects.

Just as the little girls knew how to wrap daddy around their fingers, they also knew how to get under Marge's skin. The girls learned quickly that much of the time their mother was unaware of what they were doing and they could get away with murder. When Marge did notice and attempted to discipline them, all they had to do was cry or act as though they were being abused, and Marge would back off, feeling upset and terribly guilty. It was at this point that she would try to make up and would give them more than they were after to begin with.

There were several situations where the girls knew they could take advantage of their mother. One was when she was talking on the telephone; another was when she was with them in the store; a third was when company was present; and a fourth was when she was driving the family car. On these occasions the girls had learned that their mother was too intimidated by what others might think to discipline them. The result was that they ran wild.

Bill would get home from work and would be treated to a pair of happy, hugging girls while Marge would be tense, nervous, and drawn from her trip to the store. If she mentioned the day's trouble, her husband either couldn't understand or thought that she was exaggerating. His response was "be firm." Because of the pent up tension there were times, expecially when no one was around, that Marge would really explode over some relatively minor transgression. On one occasion she had slapped one girl hard enough to bloody her nose. Her own behavior frightened her, and she was afraid of losing control and doing something worse.

It was determined in talking with Marge that she needed to increase her own self-esteem, to reduce her anxiety, and to learn more effective ways of dealing with her daughters' behavior. It was felt that if she could begin to get control of herself and her daughters in even one of the situations where they ran wild it would be a major step forward.

To help her gain control over her own anxiety it was decided that autogenic training would be the best procedure. Marge had indicated that the single area she would like most to control was the behavior of her daughters in a store. The problem in developing this control was that as they began to run wild, and as she thought about having to discipline them and about what people would think, she became too anxious to function. It was reasoned that with autogenics Marge would have a procedure that she could use to lower her own anxiety within a few seconds.

In conjunction with the autogenic training a cognitive

behavior modification program was worked out which focused on the supermarket situation. The old self-defeating thoughts were identified, and new thoughts were substituted. In addition, a set of procedures were worked out and supported by the therapist that provided some structure and a way of dealing with the girls. Through the five months it took Marge to learn the autogenic procedures she received support and encouragement from the therapist. Her self-esteem went up and so did her ability to control herself and her children.

Harry provides another example of combined procedures. One of seven children, he was able to gain a large amount of recognition early in his life due to his athletic abilities. He became all-everything in junior high and his first two years of high school—the star of his baseball, football, and basketball teams. He hoped to win an athletic scholarship to the state university and ultimately wanted to be the school's coach. However, in the fall of his junior year Harry suffered a badly broken leg in the school's first football game. Both psychologically and physically his dream was over since the injury incapacitated him for most of the academic year.

His interest in school work suffered and finally, he dropped out just before the start of his senior year. He married his high school sweetheart at the age of 18. Now his only concern was to find a job and support his wife and soon-to-arrive son.

Harry had tinkered around with the engines of his father's tractors and pick-up trucks while growing up on the farm, and when a job opened up at a small airport 30 miles outside of town, Harry got it, partly because of his athletic reputation but primarily because his uncle worked at the same airport.

Always quick to learn about mechanical things, Harry

became a first-rate airplane mechanic. He proceeded to enlarge his family by three more sons by the time he was 28 years old.

Since he was so preoccupied with his job, Harry's wife was the one who controlled the running of the house, the family's finances, and supervised her sons' activities, hoping that they would get good educations and better jobs in more substantial careers than just being airplane mechanics or even star athletes.

Harry's life was complicated by his inability to say no to the demands of family and friends. He would work extra hard to cover for buddies who would go off before their work was done and often found himself so overextended that he would fail to complete many of the tasks he tried so desperately to accomplish. As the pressures increased Harry became plagued by migraine headaches which lasted for as long as three days. At times it was so bad he was forced to go for emergency care at the local hospital, where they had tried to treat him with morphine because nothing else seemed to reduce the pain.

Harry had tried every form of medication imaginable. Although the drugs would work briefly he would soon develop negative reactions. He began to lose his hair, experienced rectal bleeding, feelings of dizziness and loss of control. It was obvious that medicine was not the answer and he gave the drugs up.

At the suggestion of one of his doctors Harry consented to enter a biofeedback program. He was very anxious about this procedure, more so than most people. At the same time he was extremely eager to please. Harry's physical problem, his tendency to deny stress and psychological difficulty and his interest in mechanics and electronics all operated to get him quickly involved in biofeedback. His submissiveness and low self-esteem, which might have interfered if he attempted a total self-treatment program, were coun-teracted by a very supportive trainer.

His biofeedback treatment consisted of temperature feedback in the initial training, and Harry was very quickly able to change the temperature of his finger. This was a positive result, since biofeedback theory says that if you can relax, you can increase the blood flow to the hands, and this subsequent increase in temperature shows that a person is relaxing. By redirecting one's flow in such a manner there is also a complementary decrease in blood flow to the major arteries leading to the head, which for Harry meant a reduction in pain from his migraine headaches.

Within three sessions Harry was able to change his finger temperature on an average of about 10 degrees per session. When he came into the biofeedback lab with a finger temperature of about 78 degrees, by the end of the 15-minute session he was able to increase the temperature to about 88-90 degrees. With this new skill Harry was able to use the same strategy to abort his headaches when he felt them about to begin.

His migraine problem, however, continued because of his inability to say "no" and the small amount of time he set aside for himself. Harry was under the delusion that if he did say "no" to his friends they would no longer like him and would probably reject him as a friend. In the past, the only way he was able to escape their demands was when he found himself incapacitated because of his headaches.

What was needed for this final problem was an ongoing type of relationship that could provide more support than the biofeedback did for treating his migraine headaches. It was decided to institute an exercise program, which would allow Harry time for himself, as well as an avenue to vent some of the pressure he felt in his relationship with his friends. Since a nearby health club offered a pool, the procedure was to have Harry swim three times a week in order to work off the anxiety and frustration he had been feeling. Both procedures worked.

For Harry, it was vital that biofeedback was chosen for therapy, because he hadn't seen himself as having a psychological problem. This preconception of his had been a stumbling block in terms of using some form of psychotherapy, which Harry would never have agreed to. Biofeedback gave him the opportunity to be taught about the relevance of stress and pressure and how it had been affecting his life. The exercise program served two additional functions: it allowed Harry to work off some of the constant physical pressure he was feeling, and also gave him an opportunity to spend some time by and for himself.

The next set of procedures illustrate how stress-reduction techniques can be used with a group to speed the learning process. In the example presented a combination of progressive relaxation and mental rehearsal was used to work with a large group of AAU divers. (This same combination of procedures also has been used with remarkable success to teach statistics to college students.)

The diving coach found himself with two problems. The first was getting enough practice time in so that the boys could learn what they needed to. The second was to overcome their fear and motivate them to try new and more difficult dives.

The pool provided for the workouts offered the use of the diving boards for only one hour each evening. With better than 20 divers, this did not leave much time for practice. This was further compounded by the fact that when a diver was asked to attempt a new dive he would usually stand on the board thinking about it for several minutes, further reducing practice time. This annoyed the coach and the other divers, and the poor kid who was trying the new dive would feel so bad that he felt like never coming out for the team again.

The coach decided that he could solve his problem by combining two psychological procedures. First, he asked his divers to show up for practice 15 minutes early every night. He gave them a very positive picture of his plan, telling them how they were going to learn some techniques for controlling their minds and bodies. He stressed that they would be able to use the procedures to learn dives more quickly and emphasized that all of their thinking would take place before they got on the diving board.

During the 15 minutes before each practice he instituted the following procedure: He would quickly point to each diver and tell him what dive he wanted him to practice mentally that night. The dive might have been one they were having trouble with, or a new one they were supposed to learn. Next, the entire squad would all lie beside the pool as the coach talked them through progressive-relaxation exercises. As soon as they were relaxed he would have them mentally rehearse their designated dive for the evening.

The coach used these exercises to create certain expectancies for the divers. They were told to visualize and rehearse not only during the exercises but while they were in line waiting for their turn. They were then to get on the board having already thought about the dive, get themselves ready, take a deep breath and go. Under no circumstances were they to spend a lot of time thinking on the diving board. If they were unable to get ready in time they simply went to the end of the line.

The results of the program were remarkable. Almost no time was wasted on the board. The divers began to learn more dives faster, made fewer mistakes because they were more relaxed, and when they did land wrong, they recovered more quickly and seemed much less affected.

These procedures lend themselves very readily to any situation that demands coordination and good emotional control. The implementation of relaxation and rehearsal in driver-training, swimming and first-aid classes have been very successful. As we mentioned earlier, the trick is to select the right relaxation procedure for the person and the situation, and to know what to rehearse.

Now for another successful application. Although Julie has her own career as a nurse she is expected to be supportive of her husband, a corporate executive. It was evident to both of them that his promotions depended, at least in part, on his wife. This demand for her involvement was a continual sore point in their marriage.

Julie's mother had always told her that a woman was important to her husband's career and that it was her job to place her husband first. This may have been due to the fact that social status and achievement had been very important to her mother. She had scrimped and saved the money for Julie to go through nurses' training with the hopes that her daughter would marry a doctor.

Mrs. R. was constantly trying to remake her daughter. According to Mrs. R., Julie's manners were all wrong, as were her interests and her choice of words. She didn't read enough, didn't dress or use makeup properly, and even her choice of underwear was wrong. After years of this constant criticism Julie was convinced it was all too true.

Julie got married immediately after graduating from nurses' training. Her husband, though not a doctor, met with her mother's approval since he had a master's degree in business administration, was a young executive on the move and came from the "right" kind of family. Three months after their marriage, Julie and her husband moved 3,000 miles because of a transfer that was important to his career. If she had insecurities before, this shift really inflamed them.

Shortly after their arrival the corporate parties started. The first one was an absolutely horrid affair and set the tone for what was to follow. Julie was dressed all wrong. Her husband was immediately grabbed by some of the men, and she was left standing alone with a couple of the other wives. The women quickly made her uncomfortable: "Oh, hello, and what do you do?" When Julie responded that she was a nurse there was a pause and then, "Oh, how interesting. Tell me, Ellen, have you read that new novel I told you about?"

Someone else might have been angered at their cold, and egotistical behavior, but not Julie. She was convinced that everyone there was brighter, better educated, and somehow better people. They seemed so worldly and traveled, and she was just a farm girl. They were caught up with common interests, none of which Julie shared. She was failing both herself and her husband.

In response to the pressure, Julie began developing headaches. They were real enough though her husband at times thought they were more fantasy than fact. She knew that it really was important for her to attend social gatherings because of her husband's situation, so she decided to learn to feel more comfortable when she went to the parties.

In describing her problem Julie presented both physical and attitudinal symptoms. Being a nurse she was an ideal candidate for biofeedback as a treatment for her tension headaches. The procedure offered direct applications in teaching her to relax the muscles in her neck and forehead. These were contributing to the headaches and were becoming more intense in response to her anticipation of having to go to a party.

In addition to the biofeedback, cognitive behavior modification procedures were used to alter Julie's notions, both about herself and the people she met. She was encouraged to become more assertive and reached the point of being able to initiate conversations that were more interesting to her. When she had a thought like, "Oh dear, I don't know anything about that; they probably think I'm really dumb," she learned to think, "Look at John—I'll bet he's as bored by the talk about books and work as I am. I'll do him a favor and change the subject." Julie's headaches disappeared, as did her feelings of inferiority.

The final case in this chapter again presents a group-oriented set of procedures that were used at a women's college which found that very few students knew how to deal with job interviews. The ambiguity of not knowing what to do, or what was expected, created for many students a great deal of anxiety. This, in combination with the knowledge that the job market was very tight, that they were in competition with numerous well-qualified individuals and that they would have to be assertive and sell themselves, proved to be almost incapacitating for most students.

The responses of Karen and Sue were not at all unusual. Both girls are reasonably attractive and competent. They aren't superstars, they just do a good job. In social situations they tend to be quiet, responding more to other people's questions and content to let others lead the discussion. On tests they do well, and it is apparent that they assimilate material fairly easily. If you had to rely on classroom interaction, however, you wouldn't know that they were learning.

Their problem, and that of others like them, was that if the interviewer does not ask the right questions (and they rarely do) the girls don't get the job. Open-ended questions, such as, "What do you want from the job?" or "Where do you expect to go in the next five years?" cause them to become anxious and withdrawn. Their typical response would be, "Oh I don't know; it's hard to say."

This type of behavior leaves the interviewer singularly unimpressed, and the company loses as do Karen and Sue.

To give the Karens and Sues a fair shake, courses have been designed to train them to sell themselves. Key parts are learning to relax (and we used progressive relaxation, though any of the procedures in Part I could have been used) and to develop skills. For the skill development we used mental-rehearsal procedures.

The program that we were interested in was for Karen and Sue. These women were not suffering from low self-esteem, since they knew that they did a good job; so an attitude-change procedure such as cognitive behavior modification would not be necessary. What was important was to identify some important things for them to attend to, and do, in job interviews. In chapter 7 we provide you with some of the material used in this type of rehearsal.

You have now seen the procedures alone, and also in various combinations. If we have been successful you have seen yourself in some of the cases we chose to present. Now, it's time to take a closer look at some basic information you'll need to know before you embark on any of the procedures you have just read about.

13

Knowing What You're Getting Into

We would be ignoring our professional responsibility if we did not warn you about some of the problems and limitations of self-help programs. As we have indicated, for most people there will be little difficulty and no danger in applying the things that we have talked about. This chapter is written in recognition of the fact that there are occasional exceptions. There are also times when self-help procedures will not be enough.

We have talked about the problems that develop when you tend to respond entirely in either a physical or emotional way. Don't make the same kind of mistake in terms of trying to solve your problems. We have presented a variety of psychological procedures for dealing with stress. It would be a mistake to assume automatically that the symptoms you are experiencing are due solely to stress. The possibility always exists that both the physical and emotional response you find yourself having might be due to some physical ailment that required medical treatment or surgery.

Before engaging in any self-treatment program you should have a physical exam and tell your doctor what you intend to do. This is especially true under the following circumstances:

1. If you are on medication and suffer from some chronic problem (e.g. diabetes, heart trouble) these procedures can alter your need for medication. You could over-medicate if your needs are not being monitored.
2. If you are over 50 years of age and physically out of shape, especially if you are going to institute some physical procedures.
3. If the symptoms you are experiencing are relatively new, and you don't have any past history of similar responses under pressure.
4. If the symptoms are increasing in frequency and intensity. This is especially true with respect to physical symptoms such as headaches.
5. If you cannot identify a link to stressful situations. This might be because you don't recognize what it is that is affecting you. It might also indicate some other cause that needs medical attention.

These are all signals that should lead you to consider outside help in the form of medical consultation. We have mentioned throughout the book that there are also some other signs that indicate a need for outside assistance in terms of applying the procedures presented in this book. In addition, there may be a need for more traditional psychological services. Let us list a few of the signs, and then we can talk about what you should be doing about them.

1. If you lack the self-confidence necessary to stick with a particular procedure.
2. If you find yourself unable to focus on a particular problem but instead jump from one to another without getting control over any of them.

3. If you have a low level of self-confidence in spite of the fact that you have been successful and people continue to tell you so.
4. If you find yourself unable to identify what is making you feel and behave the way you do.
5. If you find your environment doesn't provide the space and support you need to develop and work on your own program.

If you decide you need some guidance or long-term involvement with a professional, how do you select one? There are a great many people out there trying to sell you their special brand of nirvana or heaven. But just because people offer their services and are sincere does not mean they will be helpful.

There are numerous competent and incompetent people in every field. Friends, relatives, palmists, astrologers, psychologists, M.D.'s, social workers, counselors, ministers, rabbis, priests, teachers, physical therapists, naturopaths and osteopaths all mean well. But whether any of them has anything to offer you will depend on the specific problem you have. It will also depend on their ability to be sensitive to you, and on your ability to trust them. This means that they must be able to diagnose your needs accurately. Finally, it will depend on their technical skills.

Solutions to problems do not always require professionals, and certainly degrees do not automatically bestow competence. Independent of a person's experience and professional training, or lack of it, there are some things you should watch out for when you go shopping for help.

Beware

1. Avoid individuals who can't, or won't agree to, spell out specific goals for treatment. The goal may be as vague as to explore the problem in order to determine the best way to proceed. If so, it should be stated, and some estimate of time and cost for that exploration should be given.

2. Unless you want a long-term involvement, considerable expense, a journey without end, and often lack of any real purpose other than self-stimulation, watch out for offers to provide "greater insight," "more self-awareness," etc. These terms are fine, but ask what they lead to. "How will I know when I achieve it? How can I measure it in terms of changes in behavior, feelings, or attitude?" Of course, if you have the time and money to explore just for the sake of exploration, fine.

3. Beware of anyone who won't give you specific information regarding costs, procedures, length of treatment, their own training background, etc. There is some justification for a therapist's statement, "try it and see for youself." If that statement comes too early, however, it is usually meant to get you emotionally involved in a program to the point of being unable to say "no" once you find out the cost. It is a lot easier to say "no" in the first hour than it is later on.

4. Look out for anyone who announces that he has "the way" or who tells you within the first five minutes that he understands your problem and has the solution. He may have the answer, but if he does you were lucky. These people tend to be true believers in their system. They apply it blindly to everyone, and if it doesn't work the customers are at fault, not them. If they don't pause and listen, or recognize limitations to their own techniques, leave as quickly as you can.

5. Stay away from anyone who doesn't take the time to check whether some physical form of treatment is necessary. This is especially true if you present the problem as a physical complaint, such as headaches, even if you feel it is due to stress. Questions must be asked to rule out physical problems. It is too easy to ask a potential client or patient, "Have you had a physical?" and let it go at that.

These questions should be a routine part of screening. Anyone who does not screen individuals to determine that his particular brand of treatment is appropriate runs the risk of doing a disservice to the client. Screening may involve taking a history, getting a referral from another professional who has already done some pre-screening, and even more. The mere fact that you showed up at the door is never justification for treatment. No therapist we have ever met can be all things to all people.

6. There is no such thing as a *sure fire cure* for the treatment of stress and anxiety. Do not believe anyone who promises total freedom from anxiety or who guarantees they will help. We can say that a certain percentage are helped, but we can't promise you a cure.

7. Beware of the individual who continually tries to impress you with titles and credentials. Diplomas, certification of excellence and recognition by others can all be important evidence of a person's ability to help. But degrees and memberships in impressive-sounding societies can also be purchased.

You should be aware of credentials but also know what they indicate. An example regarding the certificates on the wall of Dr. X's office bears this out.

Dr. X offers a range of clinical services including psychological testing, individual and group psychotherapy. He will tell you that he can help you with stress-related problems.

The first certificate indicates that Dr. X was designated an "Outstanding Young Man of America for 1977" for his "Outstanding professional achievement, superior leadership ability, and exceptional service to the community." It is a very impressive wall hanging that should instill confidence in anyone.

But ask Dr. X how he came to get the award, and he will say someone respected by the awards committee recommended him.

Dr. X assumes the person who recommended him sent along a list of qualifications, but he does not know what was on the list or even if it was accurate. Dr. X is on the faculty at a university, where he functions as a teacher, researcher, and provides some clinical training. He does not know which of these activities was mentioned.

Four months after Dr. X received a letter telling him he had been nominated for this honor he received the certificate now seen on his wall. It came in the mail along with an ad telling him that for $26 he could buy a book that would tell him about himself.

The second certificate is a license to practice as a psychologist in the state of New York. This would seem like evidence of some competence, but the requirements to become licensed as a psychologist in this state, which are among the most stringent in the nation, have little to do with clinical competence. In fact, Dr. X might never have seen, treated, or tested a patient in his life and still be certified as a psychologist. He does have to have a doctoral degree from a recognized institution, but this could be in physiological psychology, experimental psychology, or a number of other areas. He may never have worked with anything more complicated than a rat.

The third framed piece of paper on Dr. X's wall attests to the fact that he is certified by the National Academy of

Professional Psychology as a Diplomate in Clinical Psychology. This does relate to his competence, however it is not required in order for him to practice. In fact, very few practicing clinical psychologists subject themselves to this examination, since it is totally voluntary.

To get this certificate Dr. X had to have a Ph.D. from a recognized institution and five years of clinical experience from the date he received his Ph.D. He would have had to pass an examination in which three of his peers observed him in actual therapy, as well as examined him about other case samples. They also would have tested his knowledge of professional ethics and the law.

These examples were taken from the wall of a very competent professional. They were not presented to shatter your confidence in your therapist, but rather to impress upon you the importance of knowing something about who you are asking for help. You are paying a fee for a service and have a right to know the qualifications of the person who is working for you and with you, professional or not.

It is not our desire to assume an elitist attitude. We personally believe that the most competent providers of human services have both some experience and training (which may or may not be gotten in the course of getting a professional degree) and an innate gift that makes them effective in communicating with others. They are both made and born. A qualified person in any field often will be recognizable by reputation. Still, there are some advantages to going to a professional for help.

First, a professional degree is conferred because the individual has been exposed to and demonstrated some ability to learn an identifiable body of knowledge. What the knowledge consists of is open for public inspection.

Next, professionals must be licensed and/or certified by states and associations. This means that they can be held liable for malpractice, whereas other therapists might not be. It also means that they are subject to the ethics and standards of their professional associations.

Finally, third-party payments (insurance) can be made for the services by professionals in most states. Fees for services provided for by non-professionals are not likely to be reimbursed.

Let us conclude this chapter by telling you some of the ways you can attempt to find out about the availability of services in your area.

Where to Go

1. The first place to go is to individuals you respect and trust for their recommendations. Avoid well-meaning individuals who are "true believers" in their own things. Find someone who is open-minded and tolerant, has some knowledge about you and what you are considering. Some family physicians, ministers and teachers fit this description. Beware of close family and friends who may be too emotionally involved with you to be objective.

2. You can contact professional societies whose members have expertise in the area you are interested in. Some important resources in the area of stress reduction would include:

The Biofeedback Research Society, University of Colorado, Medical School, Denver, Colorado, 80220.

The American Association of Biofeedback Clinicians, 2424 Dempster St., Des Plaines, Illinois 60016.

The American Heart Association. Eastern Office, 622 Third Avenue, New York, N.Y. 10017

The American Medical Association. 535 N. Dearborn St.; Chicago, Il. 60610

The American Psychiatric Association. 1700 18 St., N.W.; Washington, D.C. 20009

The American Psychological Association. 1200 17 St., Washington, D.C. 20036

The National Register of Health Service Providers in Psychology. (Available in most libraries.)

The Society of Clinical and Experimental Hypnosis. 129-A Kings Park Dr., Liverpool, New York 13088.

The International Society of Hypnosis, 111 North 42nd Street, Philadelphia, Pennsylvania 19139.

Most of these societies will be happy to provide advice, answer questions, and give names of professionals in your area. They will also tell you what their membership requirements are. Most of them are not, however, in a position to testify as to the clinical competence of their members. You would be well-advised to get names from the societies and then talk to people in your area who are familar with the individual in order to gain some idea of reputation and competence.

Another place to check for services are colleges, universities, and medical schools. These are often excellent sources of information. Many schools also offer special courses open to the public in relaxation training, meditation, Tai Chi, and much more. It is often possible to get training at rates far below those you would have to pay on a private basis.

The departments to contact in these institutions would include public relations, psychology, management, education, kinanthropology, psychiatry, internal medicine, cardiology, and neurology.

Both the white and yellow pages in the phone book can also provide information; for example, many professions offer referral services and you can use these. Depending on the particular service, however, they may just automatically refer you to the person on call that day, whether they are appropriate or not. Various meditative groups, hypnotists, and counselors advertise in the yellow pages. Again, you should get the name and then check out their reputation and credentials.

Many community agencies have their own programs and you can look into these. The YMCA and YWCA, Jewish Community Centers, Community Mental Health Clinics, Community Chest, Blue Cross, American Heart Association, Catholic Family Services, youth service agencies, and any number of local agencies provide various kinds of help.

Epilogue

When completing a project like this, the one hope is that the readers have been able to learn something that will be of practical use. What we have endeavored to do is to provide you with a guide and reference points from which you can better make your way in today's world.

Unfortunately, a very real issue is that living in our society will not become any easier. Nor will the pressures that we must deal with every day disappear. There will always be new stresses that will test our strength. This is a fact that in many ways probably makes life as dynamic and exciting as it is. Were we somehow to remove all stress, the consequences could prove to be far worse than what we ask ourselves to now accept.

In truth, we don't really want, nor are we able, to eliminate stress and anxiety totally from our day-in, day-out existence. Our goal here is to lessen its effect upon our performance and perception of numerous common situations. This is what *How To Put Anxiety Behind You* has been all about.

We can offer only so much and go only so far in supplying information and background about procedures and different methodologies. The rest lies in your hands. Reading the book is just the beginning. You must add the strength, desire, confidence, and motivation to get the most from your own life. Use our research and professional expertise as an aid, not as an end in itself.

Remember that you have within yourself the ability to change those things that you do not like, and to fortify those aspects that you are pleased with. It is admittedly no easy feat, but it is not an impossible task. Have strength of purpose; know that any individual must constantly take in and apply knowledge; and lastly, realize that if you believe in yourself you can accomplish great things, no matter what you want from your life. It is that simple.

INDEX